TRAGEDY AND

TRIUMPH

ON THE GREAT LAKES

TRAGEDY AND
TRIUMPH
ON THE GREAT LAKES

RICHARD GEBHART

MICHIGAN STATE UNIVERSITY PRESS | *East Lansing*

Michigan State University Press
East Lansing, Michigan 48823-5245

Library of Congress Cataloging-in-Publication Data
Names: Gebhart, Richard (Independent historian) author.
Title: Tragedy and triumph on the Great Lakes / Richard Gebhart.
Description: East Lansing : Michigan State University Press, [2024] |
Includes bibliographical references and index.
Identifiers: LCCN 2023021706 | ISBN 9781611864830 (paperback) |
ISBN 9781609177515 | ISBN 9781628955163
Subjects: LCSH: Sailing ships—Great Lakes (North America)—19th century—History.
| Steamboats—Great Lakes (North America)—History—20th century. | Steamboats—
Great Lakes (North America)—History—19th century. | Tankers—Great Lakes (North
America)—History—20th century. | Shipping—Great Lakes (North America)—
History—20th century. | Shipping—Great Lakes (North America)—History—19th
century. | Shipping—Atlantic Ocean—History—19th century. | Shipping—Atlantic
Ocean—History—20th century.
Classification: LCC VK23.7 .G438 2023 | DDC 387.2/40977—dc23/eng/20230515
LC record available at https://lccn.loc.gov/2023021706

Cover design by Shaun Allshouse
Cover art is image of *Henry B. Smith*., Detroit Publishing Co., [Between 1906 and 1910],
https://www.loc.gov/item/2016806453/.

Visit Michigan State University Press at *www.msupress.org*

For my mom,
Bonnie J. Gebhart

Contents

Preface

hese stories came together organically. They emerged from fragments of written stories buried in reels of newspaper microfilms. Portions languished in dormant reports that I found both online and in the book-lined walls of the Purdy-Kresge Library in Detroit. This splendid research center of Wayne State University and its narrow aisles, staid in the mummy dust smell of old books, is an enchantment. Researching Great Lakes maritime history for many years, I developed the habit of making notes or printing columns pertinent to vessels or circumstances irrelevant to my searches. If I found them interesting, they might one day be suited to a future project. Over time this collection has indeed transmuted from a compilation of facts and anecdotes into these chapters. The fragments of long-ago news grew to such proportions that they could support a story of their own.

It isn't necessary to introduce and address each story herein, but I will give brief mention to some of them. I am fascinated by the number of Great Lakes–built sailing vessels—schooners and barques especially—that traded abroad in the late 1850s. In the chapter, "Detroit to Constantinople," I illuminate some of this under-covered period of Lakes' commerce. Resurrecting just a portion of these bold sagas and rich histories is the sole aim of this chapter. In "Boneyard on the Detroit River," early twentieth-century naval lake boat designs and achievements sail past the pioneering wooden craft. In mute testimony, these decaying relics are overshadowed by gigantic six-hundred-foot, steel-hulled ore boat beasts, unthinkable at the time of the wooden ships' construction. This imagery of progress and defunctness in snapshot scenes along the Detroit River was too enticing to let slip the opportunity to write about it. In addition to some of the history of these vessels, I reference some of the people who brought these ships to life. And as these vessels witnessed time's passage, so too did these human players. "Through the Wheelhouse Windows of the *N. J. Nessen*" was inspired by a visit and overnight stay aboard the time capsule car ferry, *City of Milwaukee*, in Manistee, Michigan. And by the captivating BBC series, James Burke's *Connections*. Popular in the 1970s and 1980s, *Connections* presented historical tales through whimsical wanderings and indelible facts. When the *Nessen* was launched as the *H. Luella Worthington* in 1880, it was powered by the engine salvaged from a notorious lake boat, the *Meteor*. The first connection begins there, and the story takes us forward to today.

Personal connections shape the last chapter of the book, "The Advent of Tankers on the Great Lakes." To my knowledge, nobody has written about the development and transportation of refined crude blends on the lakes. Arbitrarily, I cover these progressions from 1862 to 1915. Had I stretched this account to 1918, I could have written myself as a participant in this story. Unsurprisingly, John D. Rockefeller Sr. and the Standard Oil Company are crucial players in the development of tankers. For decades the Standard Oil Company, and later Amoco, as it became, operated a tank farm terminal on Muskegon Lake, near the mouth of Ruddiman Creek. In 1970 or 1971, I caught one the early Standard Oil Company boats, the *Amoco Illinois*, in a mesmerizing scene. It was January, and the ship was in the channel connecting Muskegon Lake with Lake Michigan. A breakwater creates a sheltered area there, and the water was frozen over in sheet ice. The *Amoco Illinois* would surge forward, and when the ice halted her progress, she would back up. Then she would plug forward into the sheet, repeating the maneuver until she finally freed herself to open Lake Michigan. The *Amoco Illinois* was launched as the *William P Cowan* in 1918. Lacking those three years linking me to this story—once marveling at a late first-generation Standard Oil Company tanker—I offer these fascinating stories in any case.

The very nature of this book is an assembly of remnants from the historical record presented in thematic accounts. Perhaps through these stories, we may see ourselves in the unflinching passing of time. The movements of history around us fade as we age. In the reach of our own lives, we have rubbed up against so many things now silenced and lost forever.

Acknowledgments

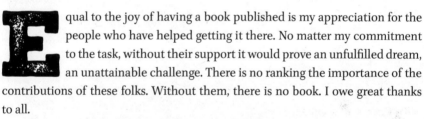

qual to the joy of having a book published is my appreciation for the people who have helped getting it there. No matter my commitment to the task, without their support it would prove an unfulfilled dream, an unattainable challenge. There is no ranking the importance of the contributions of these folks. Without them, there is no book. I owe great thanks to all.

Suzette J. Lopez of the Milwaukee Public Library/Wisconsin Marine Historical Society has long been an ally and supporter of my efforts, and I am eternally grateful for her assistance. Jay Bascom of the Toronto Marine Historical Society is always willing to lend advice or proofread, and I appreciate his viewpoints and suggestions. I thank William Lafferty for the emails and photo herein. Thanks to Stacy McCracken for putting me in touch with Robert McCracken, her husband's grandfather.

Additional photos gracing this book are thanks to the consent and generosity of two thoughtful librarians. Pat Higo, Archives and Special Collections librarian at the University of Detroit Mercy, and Don LaBarre, Special Collections librarian of the Alpena County (Michigan) George N. Fletcher Public Library.

The reliable assistance of Mark Sprang, archivist of the Historical Collections of the Great Lakes at Bowling Green State University, has benefited me once more, and I am thankful for Mark's support.

I owe a great deal of thanks to a genial man and captain who navigates saltwater ships visiting and trading on the Great Lakes today, Captain George P. Haynes.

This book could not have been completed without the technical expertise and support of my nephew, Matthew Perley, of Chicago. My gratitude for him is infinite.

I am extremely grateful and thankful for Catherine Cocks of Michigan State University Press, for believing in my stories and tightening them as needed. The measure of my success can be defined by the influences of the above named. Because of them, this book is in your hands.

The *Lady Elgin,* 1859

reat Lakes shipping history enthusiasts can eagerly point out that the year 1860 defines the *Lady Elgin*'s place in history. On September 8 of that year, she set out for Milwaukee from Chicago in a windy early morning darkness. Laden above decks with boisterous passengers and a strong contingent of Milwaukee's Union Guard in the fomenting movement towards Civil War, and with bawling cattle below, the *Lady Elgin* collided with the schooner *Augusta* off Winnetka, Illinois. The *Augusta*, as it peeled away following the collision, sustained comparatively minimal damage. The *Lady Elgin* was mortally holed. As the *Lady Elgin* foundered and broke apart in the rough water of Lake Michigan, passengers and crew clung to anything that would float as they were driven towards the Illinois shore. Nearing shore, the tumbling breakers snuffed out the lives of many as the waves by spilling them into the mad, churning water. It is generally accepted that between 250 and 300 were drowned in the catastrophe. It ranks as one of the greatest losses of life from a single vessel tragedy in Great Lakes history.

But there is more to the ship's story. The *Lady Elgin* was a wooden sidewheel steamship, built in 1851 at Buffalo, New York, a product of the shipbuilders Bidwell and Banta. It was noteworthy in size for its era; 252 feet in overall length, 35 feet in beam, and registered an impressive 1,037 tons. It was enviable and elegant, named in honor of the wife of Lord Elgin, former governor general of Canada. The 128-foot, 332-ton *Augusta*, her assailant, was also a product of New York—Oswego—launched in 1855.

Delving into the *Lady Elgin*'s 1859 sailing season reveals interesting insights and anecdotes about her cargo manifests and passenger rolls. It was peppered with incidents and provided interesting backstories from a period when there was scant photographic documentation and surprisingly little written in articles or books of Great Lakes maritime history. Captain Jack Wilson of the *Lady Elgin*, who would lose his life in the disaster, was in his first year in command of the ship. The affection for Wilson would be evident in reports in the *Chicago Tribune*, which closely monitored the sidewheeler's movements and helped burnish Wilson's reputation. Darius N. Malott, in command of the *Augusta* those fateful wee hours of the morning, was far from the Great Lakes by mid-year 1859, but even so his ship would be mentioned in the marine news columns in 1859. Ships and people far from one another in that year would be inextricably bound to tragedy the next.

The popular sidewheeler sailed for the Chicago, Milwaukee, and Lake Superior Line. Her homeport dock in Chicago was at the foot of LaSalle Street, the A. T. Spencer & Company serving as her agents. Bound for Lake Superior ports on the season-opening run of his inaugural trip, Wilson sailed the vessel away from her dock on April 12. The *Lady Elgin* was in provisional mode as she made for the wilds of Lake Superior. In addition to ninety head of cattle, staples of flour, salt, pork, lard, corn, beans, and eggs rounded out her cargo. This early season excursion to the inclement north was fraught with incidents and opens a fascinating portal on the rigors of early steam navigation on Lake Superior. Telegraph dispatches conveyed some information back to Chicago, but the meatiest bone offered to the hungry reading public came from a mate on the steamer, proffered as "Mr. Mitchell," upon the ship's return.

The leg of the journey up Lake Michigan was uneventful. At the Straits of Mackinac, the sidewheeler experienced a hefty gale and was compelled to seek shelter near Mackinac Island. The turbulent weather created havoc for a number of craft, including the schooners *Fulton* and the *A. Bradley*. In the wind-whipped, freezing rain, both boats were driven ashore not far from where the *Lady Elgin* was waiting things out.

When Wilson resumed the trip, the ship was soon thereafter thwarted by another natural force repulsive to navigation: ice. At DeTour, ice fields were impenetrable, and there the captain chose to discharge the cattle ashore. Wilson could foresee the further delay at getting his ship to her Lake Superior ports of call. The cattle compounded the gravity of the lengthened timeline of the trip, no doubt in more ways than one. The cattle had to eat, and thus, well, averting a stockyard stench seemed the most prudent move.

Mitchell's report in the *Chicago Tribune* was nuanced and detailed. By the sixteenth, the *Lady Elgin* had managed to proceed some six miles above DeTour before the heavy ice held her captive. Four days later the sidewheeler was in the exact same location. Mitchell noted the presence of vessels, some crew members of which were engaged in the rather obscure cottage industry of early Great Lakes' trade: ice harvesting. Thirteen vessels, including two tugs, were loading ice destined for cities as far south as Toledo, and in some cases, farther south still.

Struggling her way up the St. Marys River, the ship reached a point where another early season venturer, the steamer *North Star*, was locked up by ice. Wilson concluded that further progress was unlikely, so he turned his ship about and retreated to Mackinaw City. Not until May 2 would the *Lady Elgin* head for the Soo Locks, the gate to Lake Superior. Wilson and his boat had company as well. Not only had the *North Star* returned to Mackinaw City, and now joined the parade to the Soo, but also the steamers *Iron City* and *Northern Light* were intent on penetrating Lake Superior, and the latter led the way.

Frozen out at Portage Entry, the *Lady Elgin* and *North Star* called at Copper Harbor, where the latter's freight, bound for Superior City, Wisconsin, was transferred to the former. When Wilson's sidewheeler reached Ontonagon, Michigan, on May 5, they discovered the pier had been abraded by the harsh elements. Mitchell wrote, "Made LaPoint, and was obliged to break solid ice ten inches thick, for a quarter of a mile, to get to the dock." LaPoint was on Madeline Island of the Apostle Islands group. Mitchell's description of ice breaking weaves a colorful tapestry for the imagination—the sight of a sidewheel steamer on the Great Lakes bucking ice may have never been captured in a photograph. Enhancing the marvel of the scene would be the desolate, tiny port of call.

Between May 7 and 11, the *Lady Elgin* was held by ice outside of Superior City. This latest round of being marooned led Wilson to his next option for a handful of passengers. They could be returned to LaPoint—they declined—or be landed by scrambling over ice, some distance from the city. They chose this option. Hardships were burdened by tragedy in this arduous undertaking. Mitchell again writes, "There were three ladies among the passengers, and one of them lost a child while lying in ice, and they were obliged to carry the corpse to this city."

The steamer returned to Chicago on May 17. Her return cargo consisted of pig iron, hides and damaged wheat taken on at Mackinaw City, possibly salvageable cargo from either the *Fulton* or the *A. Bradley.*

Simultaneous with the *Lady Elgin*'s movement down Lake Michigan en route to her dock at Chicago, Malott could be found in a most unseemly place: New Baltimore, Michigan. Young Malott had just taken charge of the barque *Caroline.* At New Baltimore, located on Anchor Bay of Lake St. Clair, the ship was taking on barrel staves and planks of oak and pine lumber. The *Caroline*, owned by Detroiter George W. Bissell, was engaged in, as were many sailing craft of the period along Great Lakes cities, the lucrative transatlantic trade. Barrel staves and lumber—black walnut, oak, and pine—were in strong demand in European markets. Liverpool, England, was head of the destination ports, and as Malott was overseeing the loading of the *Caroline*, that city too was their destination.

As late as early June, the harbor entrance to Superior City was ice-choked, and Wilson's ship could close in no nearer than a mile. Landing passengers was accomplished with small boat or by foot over ice. The captain also reported the miserable gale force winds made sailing Lake Superior unpleasant. Off Pictured Rocks, Wilson reported that the steamer *North Star* had taken a greater beating than his boat, losing a portion of her freight and seeing bulkheads stove in. When the *Lady Elgin* arrived at Chicago, she dispersed her cargo of pig iron and barreled beef.

The scrutiny given cargoes carried by the *Lady Elgin*—and virtually any vessels sailing in and out of, in this case, Chicago—were exact. The U.S. Custom House in Chicago was fastidious in its quest for accuracy and detail. A Custom House—usually found along seaports or port cities with access to oceans—housed the government officials who oversaw the arrivals and departures of goods and merchandise. The accuracy in the reporting of these bills of lading and recordkeeping is remarkable in its precision. Hence, if an inspector logged twenty-three hogs and seven head of cattle, for instance, there is no reason to believe the numbers were inaccurate.

As a result of this meticulous recordkeeping, we know that in early July the *Lady Elgin* sailed from Chicago with 150 bags of oats, 225 bags of meal, twenty-three hogs, seven head of cattle, six casks of hams, 150 barrels of flour, fourteen barrels of pork, seven sheep, fifteen kegs of butter, and eleven barrels of salt. When the steamer

FIGURE 1. *Lady Elgin* in Chicago, 1860. Courtesy of the Alpena County George N. Fletcher Library, Alpena, Michigan.

returned to Chicago with a return cargo of barreled fish, potatoes, and beans, her time at the dock allowed Wilson to describe highlights of the trip to a *Chicago Tribune* correspondent. He declared the weather supremely pleasant as Chicago broiled. At Marquette, Michigan, he reported the harbor scene with the largest fleet ever assembled there, with a steamer, two propellers, and twenty-five sailing ships.

Summer traffic was robust. Wilson spoke of a "large number of visitors from the East." The *Chicago Tribune*, meanwhile, would recommend anyone taking a cruise away from the heat of Chicago's summer to the cool water ports of Lake Superior to travel on the *Lady Elgin*. In early August, the paper was singing praises for the boat and the man: "The Lake Superior travel has now fairly begun, and we know of no pleasanter way to spend the dog days than a round trip with Captain Jack on the Lady Elgin."

In September the mysterious movements of the hands of fate would further shape this story. On the twenty-third, a letter arrived in Detroit from Malott. The *Caroline* was on its return from Liverpool and on the St. Lawrence River when he mailed the letter. In the Gulf of St. Lawrence, some seventy-five miles from the Strait of Belle Isle, Malott reported the alarming news that the ship had collided with an iceberg. The vessel's stem and headgear were lost, but the devastation in his letter was announcing the loss of his first mate and two crew members who "were lost while cutting away the small boats."

Five days after Malott's letter arrived, the *Augusta* would have her own experience, albeit far less onerous than the *Caroline*'s. Under the command of Captain Hawkins (no first name given), the schooner was somewhere in the Welland Canal. Whereas the location is uncertain, the incident was. The *Augusta* rammed into another schooner, the *J. F. Tracy*, damaging the *Tracy*'s main rigging, rail, and bulwarks and seriously lacerating her mainsail. Perhaps not surprising, given what history would have in store, the *Augusta* sustained little or no damage.

The mystery surrounding the *Caroline*'s deadly encounter with the iceberg was clarified by Malott when the ship reached Detroit in October. When the ship struck the berg, a small boat was launched by the first mate and two sailors, fearing the *Caroline* might sink. When they jumped in, it capsized, sealing their fates. The *Detroit Free Press* report went on to tell of additional woes for Malott: At Montreal, the barque rammed a lock gate, sustaining even further damage.

Arriving at Detroit on the fifteenth of October with a very rare iron ore cargo, the propeller *Montgomery* brought news, in addition to her payload. The people of the *Montgomery* reported that while on Lake Superior they intercepted the *Lady Elgin* in a disabled state. A broken cross head beam had incapacitated the *Lady Elgin*, and it was in this inert state on the lake when the *Montgomery* came upon her. The *Montgomery* fixed a line to the sidewheeler and towed the stricken vessel to Marquette.

It is largely through imagination that we can visit pre–Civil War ports along the southern shore of Lake Superior. They were remote, primitive enclaves a great distance from the emerging, population centers of the lower lakes cities. Cross head beams were not an item in stock at Marquette, nor probably in many other locations even more densely populated. In using railroad car axles "welded" to a couple of iron blooms—malleable iron produced directly from iron ore—an ad hoc beam was produced. Said the *Chicago Tribune*, "which, for want of time, lacked finish, but reflected great credit on the mechanics of Marquette." The ship was detained for six days as the makeshift repairs were made.

The report of the incident appeared in the October 22 edition of the *Chicago Tribune*. The day before, Captain Hawkins had sailed the *Augusta* into Chicago, and the schooner may very well have been in port when Wilson sailed his ship to her dock on the Chicago River. Irony serves here because of the *Augusta*'s cargo—it carried 1,500 bars of railroad iron and 155 railroad car wheels.

On Sunday morning, November 20, the resplendent, glistening new sidewheel steamer *Sea Bird* reached her dock on the Detroit River. With her came the news of the latest inopportune setback experienced by Wilson and the *Lady Elgin*. On the sixteenth, near Point Iroquois on Whitefish Bay of Lake Superior, the *Lady Elgin* broke her cross head pin, stalling her engine and leaving her helpless, in much the same straits as the *Montgomery* found her in. For two days the ship anchored and waited for the arrival of help when the *Sea Bird* finally came calling. The *Sea Bird* took her in tow into the sheltered waters of Waiska Bay. Eight years after that dismal episode, in close proximity to the scene of the *Lady Elgin*'s demise on Lake Michigan, the *Sea Bird* would catch fire and burn to a total loss, claiming a horrifying number of nearly one hundred victims.

When the *Sea Bird* docked at Detroit the morning of the twentieth, among those landed was the chief engineer of the *Lady Elgin*. His mission was procuring a new cross head pin, which was a far easier task in Detroit than finding a cross head beam in Marquette. Successful in this, he caught a ride back to his ship on the steamer *Forester*.

While reporting this latest setback sustained by the *Lady Elgin*, the November 22 edition of the *Detroit Free Press* made note the ship had onboard "a large number of cattle and stores for the Lake Superior region." There were indeed many cattle onboard, 247 head. Naturally, there were other staples carried north by the ship, the likes of which have been covered earlier in this chapter. There were also thirty bales of hay, plus, 1,200 cabbages and fifty barrels of ale. No one was going hungry on the sidewheeler, except maybe the cattle if the disabled plight of the ship was protracted. I have wondered, though, what on earth did it smell like sailing on this veritable floating livestock pen? Did ventilation through gangways or freight doors mitigate the barnyard smell, leaving the stink of the barn to drift away over the frothy water churned by her paddlewheels?

On December 1, the *Chicago Tribune* posted a letter from Wilson, dispatched from the Soo: "The steamer *Lady Elgin*, which broke her crank pin on her trip up, above Point Iroquois, has got a new one and is ready to start on her trip." The Lake Superior destinations were as far as she would sail in this challenging 1859 season. The ship would winter at an undisclosed port, of which Ontonagon is the most likely spot.

As the *Lady Elgin* nodded away the winter in the brutal Lake Superior country through the early months of 1860, while the *Augusta* was on a lower lakes port, no one could have imagined the set of circumstances to come. Wilson and Malott would never meet in person, only the ships they were in command of would. That profoundly sorrowful encounter is one of the deadliest in the annals of Great Lakes maritime history.

Detroit to Constantinople

harles Richmond's optimism, admiring his new schooner *Dean Richmond* in Chicago, is understandable. His ship was the latest stalwart product of the Quayle & Martin shipbuilding partnership of Cleveland. Their growing prowess as shipbuilders in the period helped pave the way for an owner such as Richmond, for their aim wasn't merely trade on the Great Lakes in these early times, but the alluring distant European markets. Richmond's faith in a Quayle & Martin ship was evident in his plan, which was sending the *Richmond* to sea. Not a novel experiment overall in the realm of Great Lakes' history, but it seemed likely that the ship would be the first to make a voyage on the ocean originating from the upper lakes. The *Richmond* was modeled after another Quayle & Martin proud creation, the *Gold Hunter*, which would have Atlantic Ocean ties as well.

This account unfurled in 1856. As it did, newspapers from the major port cities along the lakes at the time—Detroit, Milwaukee, and Chicago included—were closely monitoring and reporting on the *Richmond*'s movements. There would be conflicting assertions to where the *Richmond* loaded her cargo to take abroad—either Milwaukee or Chicago—but her departure from Chicago on July 21, published in the *Detroit Free Press*, says the ship was towed from the Chicago River to the open lake by the tug *Hamilton Morton*. The *Richmond* was flying both the Stars and Stripes and the Union Jack from her mastheads. A considerable number of members of the Chicago Board of Trade were aboard as well. They would enjoy the frivolity of a ride lasting about an hour, after which they caught a ride home on the tug after it set the *Richmond* free. The *Detroit Free Press* went on, "The best judges say she is safe in any sea and could double Cape Horn with ease." The column attested to the ship loading 16,000 bushels of wheat at Chicago as it set out on its pioneering quest.

A couple of weeks later, in the St. Lawrence River and bound soon for the open sea and ultimately Liverpool, England, the ship loaded its cargo of wheat in Milwaukee, according to a report in the *Milwaukee Sentinel.* The source of this information, sent by a man who would loom large in this story, was Charles J. Kershaw. Kershaw was linked to the captain of the *Richmond* as it embarked upon the ballyhooed voyage, a man from Clayton, New York with a felicitous middle name: Columbus. Captain D. Columbus Pierce.

Pierce would play a cornerstone role in these early years of Great Lakes commerce, and his significance can hardly be overstated. He would prove a critical player in the infancy of transatlantic voyages emanating from the lakes. Pierce would sail yet another ship successfully to Liverpool following the *Richmond* voyage and would one day have a vessel named after him.

The *Richmond* was heavily insured by interests investing not only in her welfare but hopes for success in this and possible following aggressive ventures on the other side of the Atlantic. The ship's celebrated crossing, sending a Great Lakes–built ship to the historic English city, was a success that resulted in significant earnings: The *Richmond* was sold at Liverpool for a handsome price and never returned.

Of course, Pierce did. Over the winter of 1856–1857, upon his return, he was active in promoting not only the superb quality and shipbuilding skills of Quayle & Martin but also the viability of the transatlantic trade. A trade entirely based on a single wheat cargo that probably emanated from Wisconsin. Pierce, and investors keenly attuned to his voyage and experience, likely had visions of marketing goods including grains and other cargoes harvested or manufactured in the United States and North America. The buzz generated from the *Richmond*'s crossing was contagious, affecting entrepreneurs, investors, and sailors alike.

As shipbuilders undertook construction projects to seize this opportunity in the spring of 1857—Liverpool was suddenly a California gold rush—a British-built ship to American waters, the *Madera Pet*, reciprocated by arriving in the Great Lakes. The ship was owned by the Liverpool firm Cunningham & Shaw, who had purchased the *Richmond*.

FIGURE 2. Rare illustration of the *Dean Richmond*. Courtesy of the Alpena County George N. Fletcher Library, Alpena, Michigan.

The arrival of the *Madera Pet* was trashed or championed, depending on the newspaper correspondent's impression. When the ship anchored off the Great Western Railroad depot in Detroit on June 27, the scribe from the *Detroit Free Press* was mortified: "A very ordinary, dirty looking schooner with the British Ensign flying from the masthead . . . as it was apparent that no Yankee had a hand in molding of her hull, the bow being extremely blunt and only partially relieved by a heavy, unsightly cutwater."

In contrast, the July 1 edition of the *Chicago Tribune* published the report offered from a rival Detroit daily newspaper, the *Detroit Tribune*. It called the Guernsey-based *Madera Pet* "a long, low rakish looking craft . . . a beautiful copper-bottomed topsail schooner of about 200 tons . . . the Madera Pet—and a genuine pet she is—is owned by the same company that purchased the Dean Richmond. The gentlemen composing this company seem to have an eye for the beautiful, in naval architecture."

Indifferent to accolades or jeering, the *Madera Pet* with Captain Crang (no first name recorded) at the helm, was bound for Chicago. In her hold she carried a full cargo of 240 tons, including steel, iron, crockery, and paint.

In early July, as the *Madera Pet* was being scrutinized following its arrival in Chicago, Pierce was a fixture at the Quayle & Martin yard. He was adjunct to the construction of a barque of 338 tons being built to follow the route he sailed on the *Richmond* the year before on the cross Atlantic trip. This vessel would be named for the investor—a man enraptured by the success of the *Richmond*'s voyage and Pierce's enthusiastic salesmanship—when it was given the name *C. J. Kershaw*.

The *Madera Pet* loaded 3,000 hides in Chicago for the return trip to Liverpool. With yet a greater capacity for additional cargo, this disappointing allotment provided the columnist from the *Detroit Free Press* in the August 13 paper to take another shot at the British ship: "We were informed yesterday that the schooner Madera Pet would load with staves at this port for Liverpool, she not being able to obtain a remunerative cargo in Chicago, after all the bluster and 'hiccoughs' with which she received at that port."

The *Madera Pet*'s safe arrival back at Liverpool was welcomed, and with it came a most unexpected windfall. Her cargo of barrel staves took the English market by storm. This surprisingly successful venture set the tempo for a lucrative trade that several business interests exploited for several years to follow. Of the many lake boats that would profit from these extreme ventures, some would make a single transatlantic crossing, then return to lakes' trade until winter closed in. The number of vessels crossing the Atlantic Ocean would number two score by 1859. Liverpool was the most visited destination, but it hardly stood alone. Glasgow, Scotland; Cádiz, Spain; and Cork, Ireland, also served as distant ports of call. Varied though the cities and countries were, the chief payload remained the unremarkable but profitable barrel stave.

Of the bulk commodity cargoes we associate with Great Lakes commerce today—taconite (pelletized iron ore), coal, limestone, cement, and grains primarily, only grain and coal were common in the late 1850s. Cities and industries were only beginning to grow. As they did, early shipbuilders and vessel operators believed that the lakes' commerce could grow accordingly, and the world's markets needn't be unobtainable from the remote but accessible Great Lakes. Europeans wanted barrel staves. American workers were producing them. Great Lakes ships could deliver them.

Pierce knew a successful cargo as well. As the brand-new *Kershaw* was set for her first trip, a voyage to Liverpool, the vessel was laden with Wisconsin wheat. Primarily. Pierce made a call in Detroit where the *Kershaw* was topped off with a supply of barrel staves. Later, he penned a letter to Captain D. P. Dobbins, which was published in the *Detroit Free Press*, inviting him to rendezvous in the Welland Canal. They were to discuss a fixture employed on the *Kershaw*, apparently advocated by Dobbins, the "Cunningham Self-Reefing Topsail." "I will write on my arrival at Liverpool, and give you a full account of the voyage, and how the topsail works on the Atlantic," Pierce wrote. It seems to have worked well. In a brief excerpt from a letter to the *Cleveland Herald* published on August 21, written on the St. Lawrence River below Quebec, Pierce gloats about the *Kershaw*, "We are now in company of several ships. Breeze light, can't sail with us at all."

As the *Kershaw* sets sail for the Atlantic, a couple of noteworthy incidents on the lakes would involve vessels relevant to this story. On August 20, Captain Charles Gale—a rather ironic name for a ship captain—of the brig *John G. Deshler*, another new craft, wrote of being driven back by heavy weather at Port Huron, Michigan. While going in, she was struck by a squall which broke her topsail yard in two. Late in September the schooner *John F. Warner* collided with another ship, the schooner *Athenian*, off Bar Point on the lower Detroit River, carrying away the *Warner*'s headgear. Both the *Deshler* and *Warner* would cross the Atlantic the following year. The *Warner*, along with two more vessels about to come into the fold, would make annual trips from Detroit to Liverpool.

On September 8, dockside at Liverpool with the *Kershaw*'s successful transit of the broad, unforgiving Atlantic, Pierce penned a letter to the Detroit Board of Trade. The barque made the voyage from Quebec to Liverpool in twenty-seven days, twelve hours, a bit off the pace of the *Richmond*. His pride in the ship was evident: "In coming up the channel it blew hard, but the Kershaw passed all vessels," he declared. In addition he wrote that he was, "perfectly satisfied that lake vessels, properly built, are well adapted to ocean navigation. . . . I expect to commence discharging tomorrow. Have not disposed of my staves, but find a good market for them. They move slower here than our lake ports. I hope to be ready to sail the 20th of this month, and be in Detroit the 1st of November."

The *Kershaw* didn't reach Detroit that autumn, instead was forced to lay up for the winter at Toronto. Early in the spring of 1858, the ship's namesake, Charles Kershaw, according to a report gleaned from the *Chicago Press*, had lost his appetite for further cross-ocean investments. He reportedly lost money on the venture, bemoaning the return trip. Kershaw felt a loaded vessel labored against headwinds, blunting the east-bound return. Perhaps it was the undisclosed return cargo failing to meet anticipated docks and deadlines that soured Kershaw, but Pierce was having none of it.

The captain was quick to point out that a bevy of lake boats were being prepped to go to sea, intent on reaching Liverpool or some other western European port with staves or wheat or hardwoods. Pierce's proclamation of strong interest in the success of his ventures was substantiated by the emergence of other well financed players. On May 1, Augustus Handy of Cleveland entered the ranks of investors to engage in the exhilarating trade. A risk-taking entrepreneur and vessel owner influenced by Pierce, Handy had three ships to sail that spring, all with sights set on Liverpool. Three stately fore-and-aft schooners: the *D. B. Sexton*, *Warner*, and the *R. H. Harmon*, in the range of 136 feet in overall length and 230 tons. In lockstep was the burgeoning and strengthening reputation of the Quayle & Martin shipyard.

This wildly active time of Great Lakes shipping, including the awakening of transatlantic commerce, led to what is believed to be the first recruiting agency set up for these transatlantic voyages, established at Detroit, by a resident of the city and captain in his own right, A. M. Mann. Recruits at Mann's agency may have been recent immigrants themselves. Some may have found agricultural toil disdainful. Others may have simply longed for the high seas. Whereas an able seaman job today demands the worker be able to carry out functions of deck work, line handling, docking procedures, lookout and deck watch shifts, and assures the sailor of greater experience than an ordinary seaman, it probably was a literal phrase for Mann's recruits: an able-bodied man, who could work and take commands, even if he just left farm work. One early client, a captain name of Busher of the brig *Black Hawk*, reveals how sticky and perilous signing up for such employment could be. After signing on, two of the men decided a high-seas adventure on the *Black Hawk* might be more than they bargained for and quit the ship before it sailed from Detroit. According to the *Detroit Free Press*, the two deserters were returned to the ship in handcuffs. Alarmingly, imprisonment for desertion from a commercial vessel flagged to the United States wouldn't be outlawed until the passage of the LaFollette Seamans Act of 1915.

The *Black Hawk* appears to be the first vessel ever to load for a transatlantic voyage with a cargo comprised of barrel staves shipped from a most unexpected and unassuming port city: New Baltimore, Michigan. Situated on the northern edge of Anchor Bay of Lake St. Clair, the city functioned as a port so briefly that only a deep dig reveals its activity.

Pierce's celebrity would grow and be polished with a show of respect. A new barque was about to be launched that spring, slated to be named the *Cuyahoga Chief.* Instead, it was christened *D. C. Pierce* in his honor.

Early in June 1858, the *Kershaw*, Pierce still in command, was towed up the Detroit River by the tug *Emerald*, to the foot of Woodward Avenue. There the portion of her cargo consigned at Detroit from Liverpool was discharged. Earlier, in Cleveland, the ship loaded ten thousand board feet of black walnut lumber and four thousand staves. It wasn't clear if Kershaw still owned the ship and agreed to another go at the Atlantic, but the barque was heading back with Pierce at the helm. The captain's greatest concern seemed to be whether he could shoehorn aboard another five or six thousand bushels of wheat. It would be more staves, however. Along with the *Black Hawk*, *Harmon* and the *Colonel Cook* (i) (not to be confused with the schooner *Augusta* that would be renamed *Colonel Cook* following the devastating collision with the *Lady Elgin* two years later), the *Kershaw* loaded barrel staves at New Baltimore before setting sail once more for England. The *Detroit Tribune* did not overlook this lucrative trade: "Detroit is doing a stave-ing business in this way of direct trade with Europe. Push on the ball."

From Cleveland, Quayle & Martin and their stout productions were leaning hard into the ball and continuing to push it abroad. By mid-June five of their creations were bound for Europe, including the *Kershaw, Sexton, Harmon, Warner*, and the *Gold Hunter*. Others would follow. One of these ships, the *Sexton*, was so well received on its first trip to Europe (captained by T. A. Burke) that it was sold to parties who deployed it on the Black Sea. The next year Quayle & Martin ships taking to the high seas would be joined by the works of Milan, Ohio, shipbuilders and a ship built at Green Bay, Wisconsin. The year 1859 would see a market free-for-all for adventuresome owners and shippers and mariners from the Great Lakes. Liverpool and Cork and Cádiz, early, attractive ports of call for lakes-based vessels gone to sea, would give way to even more far-flung, exotic destinations.

As Pierce's star dimmed in 1859, the auras of two more lake boat captains and their respective charges were brightening. Captain A. R. Manning of the schooner *Warner* was tabbed in early April to commence his second trip to Europe. Captain T. A. Burke was given command of the *Harmon* and, at the same time, was getting set to cross the Atlantic. Both ships were loaded with barrel staves. The demand for the humble barrel stave seemed insatiable. Lake boats were loading to answer the plea. The *Gold Hunter* was loading, so was the *Deshler*, along with yet another new

Quayle & Martin vessel, the *George D. Douseman.* These would be but a sampling of sailing ships from the Great Lakes to sail on the Atlantic Ocean in this wildly prosperous time in North American maritime history.

For operators and craft unwilling to commit to long transatlantic voyage, also emerging was a viable trade to Atlantic Ocean port cities in the United States. The most desired cargo was lumber, hard or softwood. Toledo shipped several loads of black walnut to the port of Boston and other destinations, employing the schooners *Kate L. Bruce* and the *Kyle Spangler.* Ships like the *Typhoon*, a Milan, Ohio–built vessel, and the *W. B. Castle* delivered cargoes to Boston and Richmond, Virginia. But the transatlantic voyagers stole the headlines in 1859. The impressive numbers of ships embarking on these distant travels gained the attention of government officials in Washington, DC. Secretary of the Treasury Howell Cobb issued a directive in May 19, 1859, that wasn't exclusive to the ships sailing from the Great Lakes but included them:

Treasury Department, May 19, 1859

The immunity of our vessels at sea from seizure, search, detention or visit, in time of peace, by vessels of war of any foreign nation, being now admitted by all the maritime powers of the world, it is very desirable that the flag of the United States, the proper identification of the nationality of our vessels, should always be promptly displayed in the presence of a ship of war. I am directed by the President to instruct the collectors of the customs to instruct the captains in the merchant service at their respective ports always to display their colors as promptly as possible, whenever they meet upon the ocean an armed cruiser of any nation.

Cobb, a Georgian, would side with the Confederacy when the Civil War broke out. He led Confederate troops, ultimately surrendering his command at Macon, Georgia, when the war ended.

The vast wanderings of lake boats were not without consequences in these daring trade ventures. Their crews endured hardships. Crossing the Atlantic Ocean in a sailing ship in the late 1850s was a heady proposition. Skilled though these flamboyant freshwater navigators were, the mission was daunting. Newspapers published letters and dispatches from the masters of some of these crafts, offering firsthand narratives of these harrowing, and sometimes, heartbreaking experiences. One letter, from Captain S. M. Hall of the schooner *St. Helena*, illuminates the peril.

The letter was mailed from Faial Island in the Azores on November 2, 1859. Rife with nautical terms, it is edited here. Hall opened with, "My Dear Sir—I am here in a bad fix. . . . From that time [September 13] up to October 12, our sails kept going [lost to gale force winds], one at a time. . . . I have never saw such weather in my life before, in any part of the world." Hall closed his letter, "On receipt of this, please see my wife, and report where we are."

In publishing Hall's letter, the *Detroit Free Press* informed its readers what Hall could not know: "Hall alludes to his wife. Poor man—it only illustrates the uncertainty of everything connected with sea life—his wife has been dead and buried over two months." Although Hall's letter was touching, darker days were in store for the *St. Helena*.

More astonishing was the port of call a group of lake boats visited that autumn: Constantinople. Of this pod of craft, most seemed to be connected to Cleveland, including some of the return cargo. The exotic imagery of lake boats calling on an ancient city steeped in world history titillates the senses. To the good fortune of us all, dispatches and letters were recorded, illuminating these extraordinary peregrinations. The *Cleveland Herald* published the first letter, from the schooner *Vanguard*. The ship arrived at Constantinople on October 7, having "out sailed everything on the route." The fleetness of the Great Lakes–built sailing craft was reaching legendary status among their masters. The *Douseman* was unloading there at the same time, set to leave next for the Danube River. Davis also noted sighting the *Pierce* off Gibraltar.

Fittingly, the next missive dispatched from Constantinople was penned by Captain Thomas Pennington of the *Pierce*, dated October 17. The letter was addressed to "Messrs. Quayle and Martin of Cleveland," reading,

> Dear Sirs: I arrived this morning all right, and we'll be ready to leave this afternoon, I think. The Vanguard is here, and will be ready to leave the last of the week. The Kershaw went by here about ten days ago. The Douseman left here about the same time. Hoping to hear from you at Galatz [Galati, Romania].
> I remain,
>
> Respectfully yours,
> Thos. Pennington
>
> P.S. The Chieftain has not passed here yet.

Newspaper accounts and subsequent reports in the *Marine Record* help identify which captains were sailing which ships, but there are holes in the record. Captain Charles Gale had the *Deshler*. B. S. Wolvin, the *Chieftain*. J. W. Pomeroy had command of the *Gold Hunter*. When the *Douseman* came out that spring on her first trip—by comparison to her high-seas travels, a rather mundane cargo of lumber shipped at Saginaw, Michigan—the ship was in the hands of Captain J. M. Smith. It is unclear if Smith had the ship when it called on Constantinople, but whoever was in charge reported a delicious morsel for consumption in the rolls of obscure Great Lakes' history, and reported to the *Detroit Free Press*: the ship's cargo of grapes was discharged in baskets on the backs of Greek workers at a rate of forty tons a day. Not surprisingly, he asserted that the *Douseman* outsailed any seagoing craft.

By early autumn some of the long-distance travelers had returned to the Great Lakes and were transporting more familiar freshwater cargoes. The *Harmon* was working the lakes, and in mid-October, the *Warner* was logged in a marine news column making a transit from Cleveland to Chicago with four hundred tons of coal.

We are privy to some of the return cargoes as the 1859 season was drawing to a close, and the ships calling on Cleveland in particular. The schooner *Valeria* arrived in the city in October with a mixed cargo of pig iron, hardware, soda ash, and English ale, most of which was consigned to George Worthington. Worthington's name would soon adorn a lake boat, and some years into the future, his wife's name would be on the quarterboard of a steamer. The barque *Massillon* docked there a couple of days later, returned from Liverpool. The ship carried pig iron and crockery as well as English ale. Quoted in the October 30 edition of the *Detroit Free Press*, her captain, Lloyd, quite as expected given the bumptious attitude surrounding Lake-built sailing ships, claimed the *Massillon* "outstripped all her regular saltwater competitors, and did not, like most of them, employ the services of a tug."

When 1859 was torn from the calendar, so too was the zenith of the engagement of lake boats trading on the high seas. The nearly two score ships that traveled the Atlantic and the Danube River in this wildly colorful year would be reduced to a handful embarking on the trade in 1860. There were factors for the sharp decline in the transatlantic trade.

The successful trade in barrel staves was finite. It's likely manufacturers in European cities developed competitive products, eliminating the need of imports. The lumber trade is another matter but shares a common concern with the stave business—the value of a return cargo. The British Isles had largely been eradicated of timber long before the formation of the United States. Timber shipments from

New England to Europe dated to 1790. By the mid-nineteenth century, the great virgin stands of forests in the Great Lakes region, particularly the state of Michigan, were being cut for the construction markets domestically as well as overseas.

Although the return cargoes of the late 1850s—pig iron and English ale particularly—would differ from the return cargoes of coal and salt brought back in the 1870s after delivering lumber in European ports, the message was the same. There was little value in pig iron, coal, and salt—even ale—as an import, as domestic supplies were ample, and thus cheaper. Additionally, the American Civil War impacted maritime commerce.

The doughty veterans *Harmon* and *Warner* made another trip across the Atlantic with barrel stave cargoes. Another eventful saga belonged to the Green Bay, Wisconsin–built barque *Magenta*. The *Magenta* was larger than most—perhaps all—other Lake craft in service in the transatlantic trade. The 458-ton ship was but a year old when it was abandoned at sea on July 22. Having sailed from Boston, it was quickly overcome by the Atlantic, her crew fortunately rescued by a ship identified as the *Roderick Dhu*. The *Magenta*'s short life may be underscored by what went down with her in the ocean—not the 1,185 barrels of flour nor the 4,325 bags of oil cake, but the 3,428 gallons of sperm oil doomed along with the ship. It may very well be the only case of sperm whale oil lost in the sinking of a lake boat.

The records and names of many of these vessels are missing from databases relevant to Great Lakes history, languishing in obscurity from an era so long ago. For some, their demise was even more remarkable than their derring-do, far from their freshwater origins. Two July 1886 editions of the *Marine Record* recapped the final ports of call for many of the protagonists in this story, compiled by J. W. Hall.

The *Harmon* was renamed *Wavetree*, reportedly in 1865. Hall asserts the ship was wrecked on Lake Huron in 1867, but this appears to be inaccurate as the ship was listed in the *List of Merchant Vessels of the United States, 1869*. It may well have come to grief there later.

The *Warner* continued to trade on the Great Lakes for many years to come. The *Colonel Cook* wrecked at an undisclosed location on the Gulf of St. Lawrence. The *Black Hawk* wrecked on Point Betsy on Lake Michigan in late October or early November of 1862 with a cargo of 19,000 bushels of corn. It was a total loss. The *Gold Hunter* was abandoned by her owners to insurance underwriters after she ran aground near Cheboygan, Michigan, in the Straits of Mackinac. It occurred in early November of 1877 in heavy weather. The ship was a total loss. The *Deshler* was renamed *Cressington*. In October of 1863, laden with barrel staves from Detroit, it set off for another voyage to Liverpool. It was never heard from again after reaching the Atlantic. The schooner *Kyle Spangler* wrecked somewhere along the Atlantic coast of the United States. The *Pierce* was captured by Confederate forces in the opening stages of the American Civil War while moored at Norfolk, Virginia. There it was set ablaze and destroyed. Hall would also report that the hard luck *St. Helena* failed to see her fortunes improve. In the winter of 1861, the ship disappeared somewhere off the coast of the African continent.

John Martin joined Thomas Quayle in shipbuilding in Cleveland in 1854. Quayle, a shipbuilder from Isle of Man, began building vessels in Cleveland with his first partner, John Coady, in 1847, a partnership that would last two years. He joined with Luther Moses from 1849 to 1854, and his partnership with Martin ran to 1873. His three sons joined him in 1873, and they produced ships until 1890.

The protracted routes of these lake boats to distant ports of call were remarkable for this era. It provided an early hint at globalization in a nation soon to be torn apart by the ravages of a civil war, while framing the future of a waterway and marine commerce still vital today in a shrunken, digital world.

Doppelgangers to the Bitter End

I can only imagine that researchers like me, sifting through the rubble in the fields of history, at times wistfully daydream on their knight-errant visits to the past. The Cuyahoga River in Cleveland may be on a low rung of historical wanderlust—unless it involves matters of Great Lakes maritime history. The shipyards dotting the Cuyahoga were strong players in the brotherhood of vessel construction yards in the early days of shipping, floating an impressive number of durable and beautiful ships. Sadly, we are reduced to written accounts and imagination in strolling among the shipyards as little or no photographic images exist.

In the summer of 1864, shipbuilding in Cleveland was a vibrant industry. Sharing the Cuyahoga to launch their latest creations, while employing upwards of 550 Clevelanders, the firms Foote & Keating, Stevens & Presley, and Peck & Masters joined the powerhouse spearheading shipbuilding there, Quayle & Martin. There was also the yard of Ira Lafrinier, at which he employed his capable brother, Louis. (The name Lafrinier is spelled a number of different ways in newspaper accounts, databases and documents concerning the shipbuilders in publications in the holdings of Great Lakes collections, I have opted for this frequent version.) With them, and their stunning new propeller taking to the Cuyahoga, this story commences.

Accolades for this ship, the *Lac La Belle*, were effusive. In early July reporters were invited aboard the recently launched vessel and were allowed to give her a thorough inspection before she entered service. Sources vary a bit on her overall length, but most fix her at 215 feet, with a beam of thirty-one feet and drawing thirteen feet of water. She gross-rated a bit over 1,100 tons. Her main cabin was capacious, stretching 180 feet of her overall length and featuring paintings at both ends. At the forward end was a scene of Lake George, a body of water swelling from the St. Marys River, and the aft depicted her namesake, Lac La Belle, a delightfully scenic lake in the Keweenaw Peninsula of Michigan's Upper Peninsula.

The ship was twin screw, with double high-pressure engines produced by the Cuyahoga Steam Furnace Works. The engine dimensions were forty-four-inch cylinders with a thirty-four-inch stroke. Two boilers, twenty-one feet long and nine feet, six inches in diameter, heated the water. To expel the smoke produced by the ship's coal-burning engines, it was equipped with twin smokestacks, arranged athwartship. The dual stack arrangement is noteworthy. From accounts that can be gleaned, the *Lac La Belle* was the first steamship on the lakes to feature twin funnels.

Outside the engine room, the handiwork of the Lafrinier's was beautifully executed. The ship featured arched trusses on the sides, an ornate pilothouse, a sleek bow, and the twin stacks, giving it a handsome appearance. The vessel's primary owner appears to be Clevelander Robert Hanna, and he sought to employ the boat on the Cleveland, Detroit, and Lake Superior Line. Easily guessed, those places mentioned would be her ports of call. Her captain was John Spaulding, and Thomas Quirk was her chief engineer.

On the return leg of the *Lac La Belle*'s first trip, she brought down a wildly unexpected cargo probably taken on at Marquette, Michigan: iron ore. Four hundred fourteen tons of it, which by 1864 standards was a goliath load. Which is not to suggest this overshadowed the bevy of delighted passengers traveling on the sharp new steamer.

By the time the ship made her way back to Cleveland, another of the Cuyahoga River shipyards was advancing pell-mell on the construction of a remarkably similar craft. At the Quayle & Martin yard, the recently launched propeller *Ironsides* was being rushed to completion. It is just to summon the verb "rushed" in this case, as the *Ironsides* seemed to be predestined to haste. On the day she was launched into the Cuyahoga, she slid from the ways fifteen minutes prematurely. Fortunately, no one was injured by the boat's premature dash to the river, but reports claimed a large number of disgruntled citizens carped about missing the spectacle.

The similarities between the *Lac La Belle* and the *Ironsides* were pronounced. Nearly identical in length with the *Ironsides* at 218 feet in length, they also shared the same thirty-one-foot beam and thirteen feet of draft. *Ironsides*' cabin length of

164 feet was slightly less than that of the *Lac La Belle*, and her tonnage of 1,123 a bit greater. Both had forty-four staterooms, and *Ironsides* was girdled by iron sheathing over her wooden hull. *Ironsides* boasted a healthy 1,285 horsepower supplied by low-pressure, condensing engines, likely produced by the Cuyahoga Steam Furnace Works. The ship also emulated the *Lac La Belle* by sporting twin smokestacks.

While the record reveals that the vessels were near replicas in construction, they were set to toil for competing interests. Captain John E. "Jack" Turner brought out the *Ironsides* and appeared influential in its construction. A coterie of the boat's owners were investors from Pittsburgh, "Messrs Hussay, Howe, and Cooper," according to the *Cleveland Plain Dealer*. Agents for the boat were stationed at both Cleveland and Detroit, pegging her on the "Lake Superior Line." So, in addition to mimicking the *Lac La Belle* in other respects, it would sail nearly the identical route.

Unquestionably, viewed from historic photographs of these masterworks of marine architecture, they were handsome ships. From the finial carvings perched on their ornate pilothouse roofs and the graceful mullioned, radius windows below them, the lines were pleasing to the eye. The ships were comfortably furnished. Their mere presence is a telling conundrum of the state of the nation. Through the lens of opulence and elegance they represented, it was difficult to imagine the nation was being savaged by a gory civil war taking place closer in mileage than their travels to Lake Superior destinations would take them.

When the *Ironsides* tied up at the Brady dock at the foot of Woodward Avenue on the Detroit River, following a trip to Lake Superior ports on October 4, Turner gushed enthusiasm about his ship's characteristics. The steamer had caught heavy weather on Lake Superior—but, Turner stated, "She does not roll like other steamers, and is remarkably easy in a beam sea." He asserted that the ship was the best sea boat he had ever put his feet on. It was the ship's first experience with foul weather on the lakes. There would be plenty more in her future.

Further details extracted from this trip provide a look into the ship's cargoes and passenger manifests. In addition to sixty-five passengers, she carried 330 tons of pig iron and fifty tons of copper. Worthy of note, during this era, copper was shipped in both barrels and large mass portions. This and subsequent reporting on the ship's travels and cargoes would be fed to the *Detroit Free Press* by the steamer's clerk, John Gordon.

During the 1865 season, the *Lac La Belle* commenced operations well before the *Ironsides*. The "*Belle*'s Detroit dock was at the foot of First Street, a whisper from the *Ironsides*," with Buckley & Company serving as her agent. When the *Ironsides* entered service in July, she was scheduled to make eight trips to Lake Superior ports from her Detroit dock on the given days at 2 p.m. She had three other propellers as running mates, the *Illinois*, *Iron City*, and the *Pewabic*—operating at different intervals on the Lake Superior Line.

Like John Gordon, the *Lac La Belle*'s clerk, W. H. Davis, informed the press on his ship's movements and noteworthy or even mundane experiences on her voyages. In 1866 his notes revealed a new commodity added to the ship's payload: fresh fish. Staples continued to be the passenger trade and the ores and metals of Michigan's Upper Peninsula, iron and copper. Occasional loads of green hides were brought down as well, destined for lower lakes tanneries. Davis also logged by name the vessels he could identify, either in port, slowed by icy conditions, or passing in close quarters. He would nonchalantly note vessels steeped in remarkable careers and incidents on the lakes, including the *Colonel Cook* and the *Wavetree*. In late September, the *Lac La Belle* called on Cleveland where Captain Spaulding proudly presented to a friend, "R. M. N. Taylor, Esq." a forty-two-pound Mackinac—or lake—trout, caught by someone aboard the ship, possibly the good captain himself.

Operating for the Detroit & Milwaukee Railroad, the beamy sidewheel steamer *Milwaukee* arrived at Detroit on November 17, 1866. She unloaded freight at the company's dock before crossing the river to further divest cargo at the Great Western Wharf at Windsor, Ontario. Once finished, the sidewheeler recrossed the river and entered a dry dock for overhaul. The timing of the *Milwaukee*'s departure following repairs would profoundly impact the serenity of sailing on the *Lac La Belle*.

The *Milwaukee* was floated out of dry dock on November 22, whereupon she took on bunker coal for her return to Milwaukee. The following evening it was upbound, some distance above the St. Clair Flats—the delta where the St. Clair River and Lake St. Clair mingle. Precisely *where* is uncertain, but what is certain is that the downbound *Lac La Belle* was in the same area, charging ahead at full speed. Whether through a misunderstanding of whistle signals or a momentary lapse of sound sailing and the fact that the *Milwaukee* was also sailing at full speed, they collided.

The ensuing reports issued by the respective captains—Spaulding was still in command of the *Lac La Belle*, and Captain Trowell of the *Milwaukee*—were conflicting. What they agreed on was that the *Milwaukee* cleaved into the *Lac La Belle* some forty feet, just abaft the wheelhouse on the port side. The *Lac La Belle* sank to the bottom in a matter of minutes. With the exception of two unfortunates, the ship was evacuated to the *Milwaukee*. Chief engineer James Evans was lost, as was headwaiter Henry Rudd. Evans didn't escape the engine room, and Rudd was impaled as he dined in the crew's mess. He had been born under a bad sign. Nine months before meeting his end on the *Lac La Belle*, he was employed on the propeller *Meteor*, which speared the steamer *Pewabic* on Lake Huron, resulting in terrible loss of life when the *Pewabic* sank like a cast-iron skillet.

Spaulding's telegram to owner Hanna shortly after the collision was thus: "Detroit, Nov. 24—The water is two feet on the cabin floor. Probably can be raised. Have seized the Milwaukee. Shall send a boat this afternoon to save what we can." Exactly what "seized" means is unclear. Once docked and survivors of the sunken boat landed, Spaulding may be referring to beginning the maritime law protocols.

Other accounts claimed the *Lac La Belle* was submerged to her hurricane deck, and it can be determined that the ship was on the bottom in American waters. A few days later, the *Detroit Free Press* published a revealing account of the steamer's plight. The correspondent was impressed with the clarity of the St. Clair River water, as he could peer into the submerged ship:

> The cold, swift waters of the St. Clair, gurgling through the richly-furnished cabins, the heavy damask curtains dripping their festoons in its eddies, the piano open (just as Mrs. Williams left it), the rich crimson-colored chairs, sofas and every other species of furniture all floating about indiscriminately.

Pianos would become thematic in this story.

With winter soon setting in, there would be no salvage attempts until the following spring. Many expressed doubts regarding the viability of raising the forlorn boat altogether. *Lac La Belle*'s owners abandoned her to the insurance underwriters.

Whatever the value of the ship, the value of the *Lac La Belle*'s cargo ensured that some kind of salvage operation would take place, and the vessel emerging to undertake the expedition was the wrecking steamer *Magnet*. A sidewheeler, the *Magnet* had wide paddlewheel boxes and a topside wrecking apparatus, and was among the first wrecking steamers to ply the lakes. On June 1, 1867, under command of Captain Robertson, the wrecker docked at Detroit with five tons of copper recovered from the sunken steamer. A quirky sidebar in this episode was another portion of the *Lac La Belle*'s cargo salvaged: seven barrels of whitefish, reportedly "raised in good condition." It is unclear if anyone chose to consume any of the fish, then seven months old. By mid-month another twenty-three tons of copper, earmarked for various consignees, had been raised and dispatched to the respective parties. Robertson and his *Magnet* concluded salvage operations by August 1. Three more barrels of copper and a trunk containing an entire family's apparel were unloaded that day. Robertson informed the press that the owners of the clothes could claim them at his ship's dock.

Around the same time, Turner was sailing the *Ironsides* back to Cleveland upon completion of a vigorous campaign called the "Grand Excursion." The elegant *Ironsides* was flaunted in this month-long, 2,500-mile cruise originating from Cleveland and bound for the remotes of Georgian Bay and the wilds of Lake Superior. Enormously expensive, tickets went for prices ranging from $200 to $600, the latter for a first-class stateroom. These dollar figures would translate roughly to $3,700 to $11,000 today. Hardly a blue-collar cruise, it was patrician, for a segment of the populace convivial and with deep pockets. Cows were trundled aboard for fresh milk. Cattle too, for fresh meat, butchered at sea. The excursion was a rousing success for Turner and his ship. Upon completion of the protracted trip, seventy-four of the one hundred passengers presented a signed letter of testimonial to the captain "in recognition of your capacity as a sailing master and urbanity as a gentleman."

The next trip for the *Ironsides* was a special junket to Port Stanley, Ontario, and her image as a buttoned-up, blueblood steamship was put to the test. Folks going on this trip were dead set on partying. After Papsworth's Band entertained until midnight, "dignity and grey hairs did not prove invulnerable to the seductive charms of Papworth's sweet strain"; an unidentified woman took over the ship's piano and pounded away, carrying the party onward into the late hour, reluctant for the festivities to stop. When they did, most of the revelers not having staterooms, crashed on deck. Wrote the scribe from the *Cleveland Plain Dealer* in the August 8 edition, along for the trip, "One had to describe the most meandering course to pass from one end to the other. The bodies of men and women, as they lay strewed about in every position might well suggest a battlefield before the slain and wounded were removed."

While uncertainty continued to wash over the *Lac La Belle* like so much St. Clair River water, changes were coming for the *Ironsides* in 1868. Turner remained in charge, but ownership changed hands. In the spring, the ship was purchased by Captain Dwight Scott of Cleveland. His intention was to employ the vessel on the newly formed Commercial Line of steamships, plying between Buffalo and

Chicago. The propeller's many heralded trips to the gelid waters of Lake Superior would come to an end.

Scott's spring, once auspicious, collapsed in mid-June. The *Ironsides* was seized at Milwaukee, a new port of call on her new run, when he filed for bankruptcy. Unable to satisfy creditors and with legal proceedings swirling and investors pursuing indemnity, Scott lost control of the ship.

In 1869, a young Milwaukee entrepreneur, Nathan Engelmann, intervened in the saga of not only the *Ironsides* but also the *Lac La Belle*. In partnership with his brother Michael, he had forged a contract with the Detroit & Milwaukee Railroad to haul freight and passengers across Lake Michigan from Milwaukee to Grand Haven, Michigan. A propitious purchase by the Engelmanns, the *Ironsides* became the central feature in their cross-lake operation.

Still submerged in the St. Clair River, the *Lac La Belle* was generating renewed interest. By late July, the New York–based Coast Wrecking Company equipment was poised over the propeller. Her upper works were gone by then. So too were her pioneering twin smokestacks. The engineer in charge of the project, identified only as "Mr. Merryman," was extremely confident in his and the company's chances for raising the sunken ship. By early August, four of nine pontoons had been sunk to execute the raising of the ship. Late in August, the ship was refloated. With this came a macabre tale. Evans's skeleton was discovered, and not in the engine room of the ship, but forward. Astoundingly, his remains were unceremoniously pitched overboard. This would elicit acrimony from the *Detroit Post* when a reporter learned that the poor man was not being accorded a Christian burial. "We had hoped that Dame Rumor, according to custom, had spoken slanderously, but it turns out for once she has told the truth." There was no mention of the remains of Henry Rudd.

On August 30, the *Lac La Belle* was towed to the Campbell, Owen & Company's dry dock on the Detroit River. The *Detroit Post* reported that the boat looked better than expected, not mentioning what expectations were. The propeller was up for auction, and on September 21, Nathan Engelmann purchased it for $23,500. *Lac La Belle*, like the similar steamer *Ironsides*, was going to serve on Lake Michigan, and for her too, Lake Superior would become a memory.

Employment with the Engelmann Transportation Company loading and unloading the doppelganger Cleveland boats was demanding, onerous work. It was still years before ships would ferry entire rail cars across Lake Michigan, and the sheer amount of tonnages to be moved before the boxcar era was colossal. The

FIGURE 3. *Lac La Belle* at the Engelmann dock in Milwaukee. Courtesy of the Alpena County George N. Fletcher Library, Alpena, Michigan.

contract commitments made by the Engelmann's insured that both propellers would work feverishly. They would not only open the navigation season on Lake Michigan but also close it. Only at the season's end, when ice grew impenetrable would the steamers rest the hyperborean sleep of Great Lakes winter. When spring began to show signs of seasonal change, the boats would be back to work. Among the accessories on their operational checklists were a supply of wooden planks. If marooned in ice and unable to make fast to a dock, a makeshift sidewalk of lumber slabs would be positioned over the troublesome ice for foot traffic. Early travel on the Engelmann boats wasn't for the faint-hearted.

Nathan Engelmann was a young man when he died of tuberculosis at thirty-four on March 3, 1872. His early passing would spare him from witnessing the disasters his boats had in store for them. Brother Michael would not be.

Near the autumnal equinox of that year, Lake Michigan exhibited the darkness of her mood swings. *Ironsides* was under the command of Captain Saveland (no first name recorded) and departed Milwaukee at the inconvenient sailing time of midnight, bound for the eastern lake port terminus of Grand Haven. Unappealing weather deteriorated as the boat was midway across the lake, setting it to rocking. About forty miles north of Chicago, the steamer *Muskegon* was getting roughed up enough that her captain turned about and headed back to Chicago. Growing seas were plucking lumber from schooners, including the *Hamilton & Jones*, and sails were being ripped to kite tails as damage mounted to others, including the *Magnolia, J. B. Newland*, and *H. W. Hawkins*.

As the *Ironsides* pitched and rolled and belched streaks of wind-blown coal smoke, furniture and cabin appointments were upended and smashed to her decks. One casualty was her salon piano. It was likely the same instrument that entertained the partygoers five years earlier on the cruise from Cleveland to Port Stanley. When the ship safely reached Grand Haven, a number of schooners with partial deck loads of lumber were already in port. Saveland remarked on how much lumber his ship had sailed through before making fast at her dock.

Lake Michigan's inimical disposition that early autumn was protracted. On October 1, *Ironsides* was beset by more foul weather, beating her way back to Milwaukee with a pronounced list, the effect of suffering a dangerous shift to her cargo. The Engelmann boat wasn't alone, for that moment anyhow, in temporarily evading its fate in Lake Michigan's crosshairs of mayhem. The schooners *Mary L. Higgie* and the *Orphan Boy*, which Lake Michigan would one day claim as victims, were stressed by weather and damaged in the same howling blow.

At 9 p.m., October 12, Captain H. W. Thompson was at the helm when the *Lac La Belle* pulled away from her dock at Milwaukee, bound for Grand Haven. She left port trailing the Goodrich Transportation Company's steamer *Sheboygan*, which was likewise headed across the lake. There were approximately twenty-three passengers and a crew of thirty-two. Her cargo was diverse: bushels and bags of barley, barrels of flour and pork, twenty-five barrels of whiskey and several hundred tons of sundry freight. The weather was less than desirable. A bit of sea was working, taunting the ship, but not threatening it. For the time being. One of the passengers was J. E. Dowe, an agent for the Engelmann's Grand Haven office. He visited with Thompson in the latter's quarter not long after the boat left port. The captain grudgingly conceded to Dowe he felt they were in for a rough and tumble cross-lake journey, to which Dowe said he smiled and quipped, "Let her rock. We're here first."

The *Lac La Belle* did indeed rock. In comparison to severe storms recorded in the history of Lake Michigan up to that time, the weather conditions may not have been legendary, but in truth, the newspapers were in the early stages of documenting the power of Great Lakes storms. Concerning the ship, a few hours out from Milwaukee and making thwarted progress, it developed a troubling leak. Upon being alerted to this perilous situation, Thompson directed that freight be thrown overboard. He was also aware that the boat's pumps were losing the battle to expel the inundation; waves were rolling aboard. It was soon apparent to Thompson that the battle to lighten the slowly sinking propeller was fruitless. He had the ship turned back to Milwaukee, but it was much too late. Early the next morning, roughly twenty miles off Racine, Wisconsin, he ordered the ship abandoned.

In the confusion and terror of fleeing a sinking ship in rough weather, observations, even from eyewitness accounts, were understandably inconsonant. Being the last to leave along with three other crewmen in a small boat, Thompson directed who would oversee two lifeboats and a couple of yawls. As this nightmare was unfolding around them, order appeared to prevail, and initially, as the ship settled stern first into the boiling lake, all five boats were in view of one another. They were quickly separated, and each fending for themselves, scattered windblown and sea-tossed in different directions, and all likely praying or hoping for the Wisconsin shore.

Women passengers congregated together in one lifeboat, apparently charge of the ship's cook, William Monroe. We are not privy to Mrs. Smith's first name, but we know her husband, Whipple, would not survive the disaster. Mrs. Smith had no way of knowing this at the time, but what she was delirious over was being separated from her young son. The cook successfully brought the lifeboat to safety on the Wisconsin shore. Praise was heaped on him, which he sidestepped, telling the press that Thompson had ordered him to stock the lifeboats with biscuits and as many blankets that he could gather.

The *Lac La Belle*'s purser, William Sanderson, helped in successfully landing another boat at Racine with seven others aboard. His calm resolve and orderly protocols fed valuable information to authorities and the press in the immediate aftermath of the disaster. The schooner *Floretta* picked up Dowe's boat, with nine others aboard, off Evanston, Illinois, and landed in Chicago. Dowe told reporters that the last thing anyone saw of the doomed *Lac La Belle* was the carved figure of the Goddess of Liberty, which had been mounted atop the boat's pilothouse roof amid small celebration the previous fourth of July. "The figure was floating in an even position and the flag flying in the wind," the *Chicago Inter-Ocean* declared.

Fireman A. Starkweather's boat with eleven passengers was rescued in lower Lake Michigan by the schooner *Kate L. Bruce.* Among them was the ship's headwaiter, Jake Wall. Forced into action trying to lighten the boat before it went down, he wrestled flour barrels over the side. A sticky mess but eternally grateful, he would later say, "I stand there, pushing out flour barrels, and I was all dough from head to foot."

Thompson and three others in the smallest boat managed to land near Milwaukee, adding to the remarkable storylines. One of the first to greet Thompson was an acquaintance of his and a fellow captain, G. W. Read. Read said his compatriot seemed confused, perhaps delirious as he recounted the horrible experience. Thompson was anguished by those lost on the steamer including passengers who refused to leave the sinking ship as well as crew members not accounted for. He seemed transfixed, gazing out on the unsettled waters of Lake Michigan. Perhaps by then Thompson had seen all he could endure. On May 1, 1868, as captain of the propeller *Governor Cushman*, a popular Lake Superior steamboat as the *Lac La Belle* once was, a boiler explosion at Buffalo destroyed the ship, taking the lives of eleven of his crewmen. He and his wife survived, but perhaps that memory and the loss of the *Lac La Belle* temporarily traumatized him too deeply to act coherently.

The accounts of the number of lives lost on the *Lac La Belle* vary slightly; perhaps nine in all, for the passenger total is slightly different in the reports. One of the few good news stories from the disaster is that Mrs. Smith was reunited with her child. The Engelmann Transportation Company made it clear it would cover the burial expenses of any victims recovered. In early November at Racine, furniture and wreckage came ashore. So did the musical instrument threading the doppelganger's saga, the *Lac La Belle*'s piano. Additionally, on the beach near Racine the carved Goddess of Liberty from the ship's wheelhouse roof was found. Upon learning of the recovery of the artifact, Michael Engelmann instructed that it be forwarded to him at Milwaukee.

There was light fog wafting over Lake Michigan on November 11 as the *Ironsides* was nearing Milwaukee. Ahead, Saveland could see the schooner the steering pole of his ship was pointing at. When he attempted to summon the engine room to check the ship's speed, the bell wires parted. Turning the wheel hard over proved ineffective and the *Ironsides* rammed the sailing ship forward, inflicting a heavy blow, cutting her quick and causing her to take on water. The *Ironsides* was largely undamaged, the sailing ship survived, but the collision was ironic. The vessel the *Ironsides* struck was the *Floretta*, the very ship that had rescued one of the lifeboats filled with survivors from the *Lac La Belle* a couple of weeks earlier.

FIGURE 4. Propeller *Ironsides*. Courtesy of the Alpena County George N. Fletcher Library, Alpena, Michigan.

The year 1872 was Saveland's last season as master of the *Ironsides*. There is no evidence to suggest the collision with the *Floretta*—which incurred a healthy $3,000 bill from the Wolf & Davidson Shipyard at Milwaukee—was instrumental in his replacement.

Reports indicate the winter of 1872–1873 on the Great Lakes was savage. Spring navigation was rigorous. Ice was persistent in Milwaukee harbor late into April, by which time the *Ironsides* was back at work. Her new captain was Harry Sweetman, and he witnessed the use of the boat's wooden planks to land passengers. By April 24, the ship had barely budged, and so the crew placed them over the ice clogging the harbor, allowing passengers weary of delay to walk back to the dock. A couple of days later, along with the steamer *Messenger* and a couple of unidentified sailing vessels, the propeller finally slogged her way out on Lake Michigan. Two days after that, encapsulated by ice and nearly in tandem with the *S. C. Baldwin*, she began drifting out to sea. At last, she conquered the ice entrapment and resumed a semblance of normal navigation.

The summer of 1873 was insouciant for the boat and Sweetman. As the season waned, the *Ironsides* was tied to her dock at Milwaukee on September 14, and stevedores wheeled her cargo through gangways into her hold. It was a typical load for the ship: 500 barrels of flour, 12,000 bushels of wheat, 110 barrels of pork, and assorted goods. At nearly 10 p.m., the boat departed Milwaukee. The passenger complement was small: twenty-five, including Sweetman's wife. A slightly larger number of people comprised the ship's crew. As the night wore on and the boat plodded her way to Grand Haven, winds began whistling out of the southwest, the prevailing direction over the lake. They continued to grow stronger, and as they did, so came the building seas. Throughout the night, now rocking considerably, the *Ironsides* held her own. When daylight came, it revealed Lake Michigan's redoubtable, storm-wracked countenance. Waves were punching the ship, like a giant pugilist. Sweetman was experiencing the malicious temperament of the big lake his predecessor Saveland had.

Just before 8 a.m. as the ship came close enough to identify the shoreline at Grand Haven, Sweetman and his crewmen could see that thundering waves were sweeping the piers and harbor entrance, but they could also discern the spars and hulls of schooners that failed to gain the port entry. Five ships beached that horrible morning at Grand Haven, the *Magnolia*, *C. C. North*, *C. E. Butts*, *Golden Harvest*, and the *Apprentice Boy*. It was a similar situation just north at Muskegon and the entrance to White Lake, where even more vessels were flung upon the beach. With little or no chance of getting the *Ironsides* through sea-obscured piers at Grand Haven and too great a chance seeing his boat driven onto the beach like the schooners already there, Sweetman turned the boat back to the hellish, open waters of the lake.

Along the beach at Grand Haven, a throng of people had assembled to marvel at the lake's fury and inspect the damage already done. They observed the *Ironsides* as it steered away, back into the roiling waters of the lake. Around 9:30 that morning, they noticed that smoke was no longer pouring from those trendy twin smokestacks. The punishment endured by the ship had taken its toll. Seams in her planking opened, allowing the broadsides of water to enter, and the incoming torrents extinguished her boiler fire. The crippled *Ironsides* was now wallowing helplessly, and the death knell was coming.

Sweetman directed second mate, Al Pitman, to gather passengers for evacuation in the ship's lifeboats. Shocked but silent and orderly, they donned inferior quality life preservers, and set about departing the doomed vessel. As the boats rowed away, with Sweetman's the last to leave the scene, the legend of *Ironsides*' first mate Mike Crosson unfolded. He was observed clinging to the top of the ship's foremast and waving frantically for help as the ship was sinking beneath him. Predictably, the propeller sank stern first, just as the *Lac La Belle* had. The mast-perched Crosson was eventually hauled aboard the lifeboat steered by the *Ironsides'* second engineer, George Cowan. More astounding than Crosson's rescue was the story of another man in the lifeboat, John Gee of Whitehall, Michigan. Amazingly, Gee had survived the sinking of the *Lac La Belle* the year before in the Starkweather boat.

Five boats succeeded in getting away from the ship. The first, containing most of the female passengers, capsized almost immediately, drowning all but one person. Sweetman's boat overturned shortly after its departure from the *Ironsides*, dooming all aboard. The small Engelmann propeller *Lake Breeze* made a gallant effort to assist in the rescue attempt. It was immediately brutalized by the wild Lake Michigan seas, stonewalling the small ship and compelling it to drop anchor outside the channel mouth. There was a bitter twist to the *Lake Breeze*'s cameo role. The boat's first mate, Henry Hazelbarth, had been on leave from his post, getting married in Illinois four days earlier. Both he and his new bride were on the *Ironsides*, and victims of the catastrophe.

On the beach, citizens had strung out for nearly two miles, pulling from the raging surf both the living and the dead. Two more boats overturned, spilling their human contents in the surf that dark morning. Surviving passenger F. N. Ripley was quoted, "We were all washed out of the boat in which I was placed, when within thirty rods of shore, but were rescued by those on the beach in a most gallant way." Survivors were provided "clothing, brandy and other comforts."

Overwhelming grief met the end of the ship. Among those lost was a passenger Mrs. Valentine, and her small boy, Harry. Possibly named after his father, the boy had been dressed in a blue sailor's suit for his trip across the big lake, and in death, "He was neatly dressed; had light hair, blue eyes, and a beautiful, intelligent face, which, except for its paleness, looked as though he had fallen quietly asleep."

The rescuers packed the bodies of victims in ice as they awaited positive identification and claim by next of kin. One of the earliest arrivals in this grim process at Grand Haven was Mr. Valentine—who was grief stricken while making arrangements for the transportation of his wife and son's bodies back to Milwaukee. Alert to Valentine's anguish, a scribe from the *Chicago Tribune* on September 16 wrote, "It was a scene that would have touched the hardest heart. . . . It is a scene that many of our citizens have never before witnessed,—wish never to see again."

The remains of the Valentines, as well as those of Sweetman and chief engineer Robert McGlue and others, made the somber trip back to Milwaukee aboard the steamer *Saginaw*. Numbers vary, but at least twenty lives were lost in the tragedy.

A coroner's inquest was held to investigate whether anyone aside from the storm was to blame. Immediately after the ship settled to the bottom of Lake Michigan, reports of her unseaworthiness were bantered about. Stories circulated that on the previous trip some three feet of water had accumulated in the engine room. Even if these rumors were perfidious or mendacious, the shocking loss of the ship and heavy loss of life warranted scrutiny.

A mere week after the *Ironsides* sailed on her last voyage, Peter J. Ralph, supervising inspector of vessels of the 8th District—which comprised the Lakes Huron, Superior, and Michigan—impaneled a body of inspectors and experts to investigate the loss. Milwaukeeans William H. Wolf and William Fitzgerald were called to testify as were survivors and crew members. Ralph's committee spent a little over five weeks investigating and interviewing. When they rendered their report in early November, finds showed that the *Ironsides* was not only entirely seaworthy, but she was also only half loaded, dispelling any notion the boat may have been too deeply laden. The report pinned the loss of the boat squarely on Sweetman. His bad seamanship, they wrote, caused the loss when he failed to steer the *Ironsides* north for the "shelter" of the Manitou Islands of Lake Michigan, well over one hundred miles north of the scene of her demise.

The excoriation of Sweetman rings unjustly, a scathing judgement a silenced man could never defend. Perhaps the last word on the outcome of the investigation, as it appeared in the *Chicago Tribune* on November 4, captures the bottom line: "This document will probably settle insurance matters, no payments yet been made by the companies."

Fraught sorrows and proof again of the small, dangerous world shared by Great Lakes ships and their crews, the *Lac La Belle* and the *Ironsides* are worthy entries in the chronicles of doom and despair.

There is one more oddity to add to the saga. Ralph would one day have a lake boat named for him—a new steamer in 1899, the *P. J. Ralph*. Perhaps it would come as no surprise, given Ralph's censure of Sweetman for not running for the Manitou Islands with the *Ironsides*, that his namesake would one day wreck off South Manitou Island during a storm on Lake Michigan.

The Ice-Bucking Steamship *Aurania*

A large ice pack on Whitefish Bay of Lake Superior commands the attention of any ship captain, even with his ship underfoot. Imagine then, on April 29, 1909, the mind-numbing set of circumstances confronting Captain Robert C. Pringle. Captive in a field of ice several miles in size, he and his crewmen were on foot. The ship they had been on, the steamer *Aurania*, steel-hulled and loaded with coal, had sunk to the bottom of the bay.

Mangled by the ice's powerful grip, the *Aurania*'s seams opened. Water pouring in doomed her. After abandonment and watching it disappear below the surface of the water, Pringle's concern for his crewmen overarched the astonishing loss of their ship they had just witnessed. If they survived—a couple of miles distant there was another freighter trapped in ice they sought to reach—Pringle was convinced that his lost vessel's owner, John Corrigan, would be delighted in the crew's survival. Corrigan, a businessman to whom size mattered, would surely have a heart as large as the hole opened in the hull that sank his ship.

Corrigan was not a Texan. But he might have been influenced by the state's braggadocio about the size of everything in Texas when it came to lake boats he possessed. He owned the *David Dows*, for instance. The *Dows* was the only five-mast schooner ever built on the Great Lakes, and correspondingly, the largest ever as well. He too owned the lengthy, powerful *Aurora*, the largest wooden-built steamer on the lakes in its heyday. It should be unsurprising, in view of these possessions, that when the steel-hulled schooner *Aurania* sat atop the ways awaiting its launch at South Chicago on August 31, 1895, it too would be great of size.

Referring to the *Aurania* as a schooner is a misnomer, really, for the role of the ship was not to hoist sails; it was a barge designed to be towed behind a steamer. The phrase schooner or "steel schooner" clung to the vessel for her first years of operation anyhow. Its overall length of 355 feet made it the longest of the debuting class of 351-foot steel wonders. Corrigan's craft was slightly over forty-four feet in beam and drew twenty feet of water. On the windy, lousy weather day of its launch, the christening honor went to Miss Etta Corrigan. Exactly what Miss Corrigan's relationship to the owner was didn't make the newspaper account of the event, only the observation that the miserable weather subdued the normal celebration.

The size of the *Aurania* wasn't the only particular that interested inquisitive marine reporter of the *Detroit Free Press* when writing about Corrigan's monstrosity. He pointed out that the three pole-shaped spars on the barges' deck were not designed to nor did they carry sails. Rather, they were strung with lights and rigged with apparatus for maneuvering grain elevator spouts and similar tasks. It had a forward bridge and a steering wheel, a rare feature on a tow barge. The deck was long and clear of a deck house or other obstruction and had a donkey boiler situated aft on the vessel. Combined with a tall, cylindrical funnel poised over her aft cabin containing her crew's quarters, the *Aurania* could easily have been mistaken for a modern, stretched-out steamboat. Rated A-1, valued at $130,000 and netting a robust 2,999 tons, the barge was soon ready for service. Corrigan would pair it with his powerhouse *Aurora*. It wasn't unusual for a new steel barge to be towed behind a smaller wooden-constructed steamer, even if the towing ship wasn't in the class of the virile *Aurora*.

The *Aurania* soon began setting new cargo records. On September 13, it loaded 4,400 tons of iron ore at Duluth, establishing a new mark. Under a month later, shoehorning in an additional hundred tons at Ashland, Wisconsin, it broke its own record. Her enormous cargo capacity was likewise shown in the grain trade. In late November, the big steel schooner was logged down at the Soo, laden with 141,000 bushels of wheat loaded at Port Arthur, Ontario, yet another huge payload.

The 1898 shipping season brought a broad range of adventure and misadventure for the Corrigan duo, running the gamut from quotidian toil to mishap and mayhem. On Sunday afternoon, July 24, around 4 p.m., the *Aurora* and *Aurania* cleared the St. Clair River downbound and ore-laden through the Flats and the channel widening into Lake St. Clair. Upbound and approaching the same location was the Minnesota Steamship Company's big steel steamer *Masaba* and the small wooden-built steamer *Edward Smith*. Surprisingly, there were two wooden steamers named *Edward Smith* operating on the Great Lakes in 1898. In addition, they were similar in size and tonnage, and marine news columns would distinguish them as "*Ed Smith No. 1*" and "*Ed Smith No. 2*." *Ed Smith No. 1* was the 1883-built, slightly smaller one, while the 1890-built vessel became *Ed Smith No. 2*.

The faster *Masaba*, presumably to make the cut to the river first, knifed ahead of the *Ed Smith No. 2*—identified by the subsequent report in the *Detroit Free Press*—to pass her. This left the *Smith* in a pickle. As the *Smith* cleared the *Aurora*, the astute captain of the *Aurora*, Andrew Gaines, could see imminent danger and checked-down his speed to slacken the towline to the *Aurania*, trailing by several hundred feet—perhaps one thousand. The move would allow the *Smith* to safely cross between the tow and not foul her propeller. It worked, but she couldn't avert the oncoming *Aurania*. The big steel schooner barge rumbled into the *Smith* abreast her boiler house at an estimated 7 miles per hour, and the impact "crushed her quarter like an egg shell." Fortunately, the hissing, escaping steam, which immediately erupted following the collision, injured no one. The *Smith* went careening in a westerly direction and sank decks to water outside the shipping lanes. No one aboard the *Smith* was injured. She was reported to have had a few passengers aboard on a pleasure cruise, most likely friends of her owner. So much for that happy junket. The *Aurora* and *Aurania* never even slowed. The July 25 issue of the *Detroit Free Press* reported on the *Aurania*'s condition, stating, "It could be seen by the dim light that her bows were well smashed in." The scribe went on to write, "The hole in the Smith extends from her boiler house almost to her keel and is large enough to drive a team of horses through." Which vessel was ultimately held responsible for the collision isn't clear.

There are several reasons for the frequency of collisions between ships plying the lakes and their tributaries. The sheer number of vessels navigating congested waterways in the early days lent itself to the strong possibility of collision. Close quarters were conducive to ships ramming one another. The odds of sailing into another boat on the open lake seems preventable on such a vast water surface, but there are considerations.

The navigational aids that greatly reduced the chance of collisions, particularly radar and radio communications, were generations into the future. Steamships,

FIGURE 5. Steamer *Edward Smith* sunk by collision with *Aurania* in 1898. Courtesy of the Alpena County George N. Fletcher Library, Alpena, Michigan.

and by extension, steam whistles, were prescribed methods of communication to sailing. Vessel masters could "speak" to one another using established whistle blasts. Hardly failsafe, this form of communication was superior to its precursor employed on sailing ships: a bell. There were also collisions due to blankets of fog that smothered the lake and rendering visibility nil. Over the history of lakes' shipping, boats crashing into each other in foggy conditions has sent many to the bottom with a grim loss of life.

On July 29, the *Aurania* was in Cleveland, and her damages had been assessed: She needed thirteen plates replaced in her bow. It was also reported that fourteen bottom plates damaged earlier in a grounding incident at the Soo would be replaced at the same time. Eight days were targeted as the time frame for completion of the task.

As the autumn of 1898 yielded to winter, the calendar belied the prevailing cold already enveloping the lower lakes—winter had arrived with fury. Biting winds and temperatures well below normal were persistent. Frequent snows added to the misery for both pedestrians afoot and boats afloat. Ice was rapidly forming in the Western Basin of Lake Erie and Lake St. Clair, creating hardships for vessels that hadn't yet gone into winter lay-up or were en route to it. It was snowing heavily on December 10 when the *Aurora* with the *Aurania* tagging behind in tow, ran aground on Bois Blanc Island, near the lighthouse, on the lower Detroit River. Both were crammed with wheat from Duluth and headed for winter lay-up at Buffalo. They were not alone in this unfortunate incident. Like forgotten puzzle pieces desultory on a frozen white mantle of ice and snow, from Detroit to Toledo and Point Pelee, boats were aground or hostage to ice in the inhumane conditions, a number of them damaged and leaking.

The *John Craig* couldn't escape the ice field gripping the harbor entrance of the Maumee River at Toledo, and the *Selwyn Eddy* and *S. C. Reynolds* couldn't penetrate it attempting to get in. The *Commodore* was aground and icing over on Bar Point. A little more than a quarter mile from the fetched-up *Aurania* was the whaleback barge 202. "The pig," as she was affectionately nicknamed in the *Detroit Free Press*, had broken away from her towing steamer and another whaleback creation, the *A. D. Thomson*, and drew attention to her predicament. She had completely iced over, sculpted in wild festoons, rendering the whaleback a creation more likely crafted from the brush of Salvador Dali than the shipyard of Alexander McDougall.

In the early morning hours of December 12, the watchman of the *Aurora* detected smoke as he was making his rounds. It appeared to be emanating from the vicinity of the steam steering apparatus and concerned him enough to warrant his sounding the alarm. The cold weather hadn't abated, and strong winds taunted and finally overwhelmed the efforts of the *Aurora*'s crew to extinguish the growing blaze. Gaines ordered the seacocks opened allowing the ship to fill, and it sank in eighteen feet of water. Scuttling the ship would save its hull.

Press correspondents and fascinated residents of the area ogled at the ungainly plight of the lake boats. Several hundred ships sailed along the river passage in favorable times and conditions, and most likely many of them were familiar and recognizable to people living near ports. But the dystopian winter scene arrested them. "The sights in the vicinity of Amherstburg are said to be magnificent. Most of the boats within view are thickly coated with ice which has been part of their cargo for many days, some of it comes clear from Lake Michigan and Lake Superior on their decks," wrote the *Detroit Free Press* on December 12. "Decks, rigging and cabins are white with ice and then a black clothed figure moving over them makes the effect all the more striking."

No doubt still exhaling resigned whiffs of smoke, the *Aurora* was described in the same source: "Burned down to four feet below her main deck, her engines are a complete wreck, and her boilers have tumbled forward into the charred hull in front of them."

After lightering a considerable portion of her cargo late in the afternoon of the fifteenth, the *Aurania* was released. Several tugs aided in the rescue, including the *Wales* and *Saginaw*. At the Detroit & Milwaukee Railroad elevator, the salvageable grain was lifted from the steel schooner's hold. Next, she was towed to the foot of Orleans Street, site of the humming Detroit Dry Dock Company. Already some weather-damaged boats had gathered there awaiting repairs, including the *Grecian*, *City of Rome*, *George Presley*, and *Fayette Brown*.

Having learned of the grim situation regarding the condition of two of his titans, Corrigan decided that it was time to swap the roles of the burned-out *Aurora* and the orphaned *Aurania*.* Perhaps with an eye to the future when the *Aurania* first took to the water, including that uncommon steering wheel in her forward bridge—we can't be certain—Corrigan deemed it a fortuitous time to convert his big steel schooner into a self-propelled steamship.

Over the ensuing winter and into the spring, the activity at the Detroit Dry Dock Company was hectic. Work began in earnest on the *Aurania*'s transformation in early April of 1899. It was halved, with plates and frames removed and her keel lifted with hydraulic jacks. One hundred twenty men toiled on the project. On April 18, her engine was placed and by early May her boilers as well on the bed plate fashioned by the company's engineers. The engine was a triple expansion unit with cylinders 17, 27½, 46" × 36" stroke. Her boiler was over thirteen feet long, fully generating 165 pounds of steam that generated around 900 horsepower.

Dry dock spokesman and treasurer Alexander McVittie expressed satisfaction in not only the punch of the new steamer and its capable engine but also its coal-consuming economy. The scribe from the *Detroit Free Press*, most likely the oft-vitriolic J. W. Westcott, was unpersuaded. Westcott, whose name lives on today

---

* On May 6, 1899, the burned-out hull of the *Aurora* was towed to the foot of Twenty-Fourth Street in Detroit and offered for sale by sealed bid. Notes in the Runge file of the Milwaukee Public Library declare her machinery was salvaged and installed to power another of Corrigan's vessels, the *Australia*. In 2012, on Harbor Island at Grand Haven, Michigan, low water levels revealed a treat for marine historians. Long abandoned (1930s) and forgotten, the remains of the *Aurora* came back to light. Some two hundred feet of ribs and keel were exposed, with ninety feet of her still covered by shifting sands and flora.

on the mailboat that serves the Detroit River, began his long tenure as marine news columnist at the *Detroit Free Press* in 1875. Curmudgeonly at times, Westcott would chastise rival newspapers and the actions of shipbuilders, vessel operators, sailors, and ships themselves when displeased. Aside from feeling the boat would be underpowered, he dipped his pen in the well of insolent ink, writing, "A little pop-gun of a smokestack, and boiler house and upper works set at the extreme after end of a long, bulky hull combine to give the transformed steamer *Aurania* about as homely an appearance as it is possible to conceive. She is not even as good looking as the whaleback steamers."

When the *Aurania* sailed for the very first time, it covered a very short distance—to the Detroit & Milwaukee Railroad elevator where she reclaimed her lightered grain cargo. She then delivered the grain in Buffalo, five months overdue. Later that summer, August 15, specifically, in irksome foggy conditions, the *Aurania* grounded while loaded with iron ore and seeking the entrance to Cleveland. It was asserted that the glare of a blast furnace was mistaken for the blinking lighthouse. Gaines, the former master of the *Aurora*, was in command at the time. He wouldn't attest to the blast furnace theory, or anything else. He was mum while the ship was lightered. No damage was incurred.

Corrigan's substantial investment in the *Aurania*, as much as $70,000 according to one report, indicate that his expectations were correspondingly lofty. Its revival as a steamship ensured she would be put to work early in the season and run late into it. As the coming years played out, it became evident that Corrigan's investment was a harbinger of the opening of the navigation season. His boat was fit-out ahead of most and sailed into the frozen regions of the Great Lakes earlier, and these dramatic encounters with the ice defined the ship's legacy.

In the spring of 1901, navigation on the St. Clair River and the lower reaches of Lake Huron was frozen to a literal standstill. At the end of April, just above Port Huron, Michigan, approximately twenty vessels were making imperceptible progress in the grip of the ice field. One of them was the *Aurania*. Also identified were *Tampa, Gordon Campbell, Italia, Amazon, Vega, Pentland,* and *George G. Hadley*. Downstream on the St. Clair River was another smattering of vessels trying to work their way through the imprisoning ice jam, some for almost two weeks. The situation was at least stable—there were no boats in distress.

Occasionally ships captive in the shifting ice would free themselves briefly, only to be locked in again. At the southern end of the St. Clair River, from Marine City to the Flats, the extraordinary spring ice bedazzled residents. So astonishing was the drama of natural elements being battled by the inventions of humankind, the region's largest daily newspaper, the *Detroit Free Press*, dispatched a photographer to capture images for its readers. Sending a photographer to shoot a scene was a rare feature in 1901. Photos in newspapers from the era were mostly portraits of individuals. It was far more common for staff artists to illustrate the newspaper with sketches and drawings; thus it was a rare treat for *Detroit Free Press* readers when the photo of the steamer *Jim Sheriffs*, iced-in and listing precariously near a dock at Marine City, was published. So monolithic was the ice jam that one of the staff illustrators drew a map of the St. Clair River for the May 1 edition, pinpointing where numerous vessels were held in ice in the vicinity of Algonac, Michigan. Included in the cluster were the *Ravenscraig, C. F. Bielman, Arundell, St. Paul, Douglas, George Presley, City of London, Pentland*, and *George G. Hadley*; the latter two had worked their way down the river only to be held captive again.

Working its way north from Detroit, the big wrecker *Favorite* was making an impact on the frozen battlefield of commerce. Alternating the use of her twin screws, she successfully gnawed through ice and freed most of the aforementioned locked-in group allowing them to proceed down river into Lake St. Clair. Captain Joe Lockeridge of the *Arundell* sang the praises of the *Favorite*. "We would have been up there yet if it hadn't been for the Favorite," he said from Detroit. "She came up here last night and we could see the fire fly when she got to work on some of the boats. She went right around them and cut 'em out. She's on her way up to Port Huron." The protracted imprisonment in ice was taking a toll on deliveries of bunker coal, and Lockeridge alluded to this as well. "There isn't a pound of coal up the river," he declared, "and the boats that are lying up at Detroit will do mighty well to wait awhile before they go taking any chances of getting up to a point on the river where they will run into ice and have to stop for want of coal." Lockeridge was interviewed in the May 2 edition of the *Detroit Free Press*.

The diminished coal bunker would affect the *Aurania* along with many others. Before the ship could retreat to the Smith Dock on the Detroit River and line up for replenishment on May 8, the *Detroit Free Press* photographer was adding even more stunning photos of the epic ice jam. The May 4 edition published striking images of the schooner/barge *Uranus*, including one taken the day after it had collided with and carried away portions of the steamer *H. S. Pickands*. The dramatic theater in icy navigation she had found herself amid was only the beginning of harrowing times ahead for the boat and her people. But before these perils came to pass, however,

Corrigan and his boat factored into the heated strife characteristic of the labor movement of the period.

In the spring of 1904, the Masters and Pilots Association (MPA), to which many Great Lakes captains belonged, had little trouble in persuading them not to return to their ships when their wages were cut from the previous sailing season. MPA was not affiliated with the American Federation of Labor, and was at odds with the powerful Lake Carrier's Association, which represented the ship owners. In this era of trusts, the definition took on broad meaning, but unmistakably meant monopoly. Silver and gold mines in the West, the steel industry, and Andrew Carnegie. Rockefeller's Standard Oil Company and railroads echoed the word "trust." Wall Street, the center of finance, was considered one. The Sherman Antitrust Act of 1890 provided tools for pushback against corporation power, but it was rarely invoked.

By organizing as a labor force, workers stood up to the conglomerates. Strikes were often localized. For example, grain trimmers—workers hired to load grain on a ship—might strike only at Milwaukee. A workforce employed in loading coal may strike only at Toledo. The MPA strike was very successful for a couple of months, literally paralyzing shipping on the lakes from the start and through the duration. The strike raised the ire of many vessel owners and inspired one veteran captain and a man with a prominent profile in the realm of Great Lakes' history, Marcus M. Drake, who took matters into his own hands. He took command of a ship for the first time in thirty years when he sailed the steamer *Chili* from Buffalo. He promptly ran it aground. Undaunted, once released he sailed it on to Chicago.

Corrigan likewise pressed himself into service during the strike, although in a far less prestigious role: he sailed as a deckhand on the *Aurania*. Maybe the result of Drake's taking command of a ship influenced his thinking in the role he wished to play. With the *Aurania* in tandem with the barge *Polynesia* for this one trip, they departed Buffalo for Milwaukee, laden with anthracite coal. When passing Port Huron, someone fired a gun at the *Aurania*. Corrigan, once the vessels arrived at Milwaukee on the thirteenth of May, described the dangerous encounter. Gaines was yet the *Aurania*'s captain. He never belonged to the MPA, and some union member showed his disdain for Gaines in the volley of bullets. Corrigan was at the *Aurania*'s stern, adjusting the hawser to the *Polynesia* when he saw the muzzle flash of one shot. Perhaps speaking with a bit of liquid bravado, he was quoted, "If I had a gun myself I could easily picked off the man who fired, as he was near enough. Fortunately, no one was hurt." The strike ended two days later, and not in favor of the captains of the MPA.

FIGURE 6. Appropriately, *Aurania* in icy water. Courtesy of the Alpena County George N. Fletcher Library, Alpena, Michigan.

Once again, it would be the story of freezing weather and iced waterways and lakes, not hot lead that defined the *Aurania*'s history. Heavy ice accumulation in the northern lakes was the rule in April of 1905. By mid-month, several boats were locked-in on lower Whitefish Bay, just above the Soo. The *Sultana* and *J. T. Hutchinson* had been held fast for over a week. Harry Coulby, president of the mighty Pittsburgh Steamship Company, the largest fleet on the Great Lakes, had personally gone to Sault Ste. Marie where he boarded the ice-breaking steamer *Algomah* for a firsthand look at the frozen waterscape and captive ships. South of the Soo, several boats were held in heavy ice in the Straits of Mackinac, while others were held in port, steam up and ready to sail, once conditions improved.

When, on April 17 the *Aurania* worked its way through an opening in the ice to Escanaba, Michigan, this success by a vessel of questionable horsepower was noteworthy for the marine news columns. They also reported on the extensive damage sustained by vessels bucking ice in this increasingly costly spring. The articles began to sound like a triage list of wounded lake boats waiting to be dispatched to available dry dock spaces. The *Frontenac* suffered twenty-four broken frames and plate damage. The *Maruba* had a four-foot hole stove in her by ice, which was covered by a canvas jacket. The *Utica* sustained broken plates battling ice in the Straits of Mackinac, and the *Andaste* cracked seven frames and two bow plates wrestling her way down Lake Superior. Stripped propeller buckets were the order of the day for many boats, crippling among others the *J. T. Hutchinson, W. D. Rees, Frank T. Heffelfinger,* and *Henry W. Oliver.* Reported the *Detroit Free Press*, "The American Shipbuilding Company is receiving orders for propeller wheels faster than it can fill them, and the men employed in the foundries are working day and night."

This body of evidence reveals the hazards and potential expense attached to navigation in ice on the Great Lakes. The *Aurania* managed the encumbrances she faced sailing in such rugged conditions for several years. Alas, the many times she tempted fate on the frozen surfaces of the lakes would one day catch up to her.

On the morning of April 26, 1909, loaded with coal and bound for Duluth under the command of Captain Pringle, the *Aurania* cleared the Soo locks. There was abundant ice in Whitefish Bay, arresting the boat's progress. Pringle could discern other boats nearby, including the steamers *Troy, Charles Beatty,* and the *Edward Y. Townsend,* as well as unidentified others working the ice field. More vessels came snorting and bulling into the ice pack only to be stymied. Three days later, near the foot of Ile Parisienne, Pringle was notified by a crewman that the ship was rapidly taking on water. The relentless pressure from the ice surrounding and solidifying around the *Aurania* stove in her hull, and the boat was in peril.

Pringle had the ship in distress flag run up her pole and began blowing the ship's whistle indicating the same. She soon began taking on a severe list, making it difficult to stand upright. The ship's doom was imminent. Pringle gathered his crew of twenty to her rail and ordered them to lower three small boats over the side. They moved as quickly as possible to distance themselves from the ship, burdened by clambering over the irregular ice configurations and dragging the small boats behind them. The *Cleveland Plain Dealer* would later say of the ship's demise, "The spectacular sinking of the great ship and the fight for life on the breaking ice floes rival the adventures of Perry and Amundsen in the far north."

Forced over by the immeasurable tons of ice pressing against her, the boat's masts were touching the ice, and her upturned keel was visible above the highest pinnacles of ice formation. Slowly the *Aurania* righted—corrected her list in the water—and for ever so fleeting a moment, sat even keeled. Then a quick gush of pressure release, and it slipped beneath the surface.

Being marooned on unstable ice in morning light on Whitefish Bay was probably the most surreal event in the lives of Pringle and his crewmen. Pringle was interviewed by the *Cleveland Plain Dealer* on May 3, where he elaborated on their plight. He estimated that they were perhaps a mile from open water, but still many miles from shore, adrift on a moving island of ice. Dotting the icescape were several freighters at various distances, including two he could identify as boats belonging to the Peavey fleet, one of scores of vessel operations on the lakes with multiple boats. Away from the open water was yet another vessel trapped in the same floe the *Aurania* had been. Pringle estimated the boat to be about three miles distant and he felt the best hope for his crew rested in reaching it, and to that end they set out. Pringle broke his crew into three parties, two with a yawl and the third party included himself and his personal small, wooden boat. "The ice was just a mass of broken burgs and cakes which had been driven together and piled up by the wind, making a great floe," he asserted.

The difficulty of dragging the small boats over the haphazard floes made for slow progress and forced a change in strategy. Pringle decided to have one party abandon their boat so that they could move faster. Should they reach open water, the rest of the party would be following them with the remaining two boats. Unburdened by their boat, the party moved ahead swiftly. It was a risky strategy. "I was afraid the ice would melt or the wind change and break up the crush and leaving us floating on half a dozen little slabs out into the lake, so I hated to leave the boats," the captain said, "but finally I decided to leave the other yawl [as well] and follow with my light boat to cross any open water or help any of the men in case of serious trouble." The second group likewise pulled away quickly. "Every little while a man would go through [the ice] and I thought the finish had come, but we made it," Pringle continued. "Made it" means they made their way to the big steamer *J. H. Bartow.* The crew of the *Bartow* had been watching the drama unfolding, and when the crew of the *Aurania* were all safely aboard, "We had a welcome that would call a man back from the dead," the grateful captain intoned.

The gratitude warming Pringle didn't lessen his anger at other ships. He had harsh words for the Peavey boats which he felt had abandoned the men of the *Aurania* to their plight. "Why the Peavey boats should have disregarded our signal and left, I cannot imagine. They were less than a third as far away as the Bartow, and in comparatively open water. Some adverse blessings follow those crews, I can tell you. If you want the real feeling of desolation and the end of all things, just watch what you think is your only chance, turn tail and disappear like that." Pringle composed himself at this juncture of the interview. He then sang the praises of his crew. "And the crew was a bunch of thoroughbreds," he told the reporter. "I don't want to see a gamer bunch. They called it a cake walk, and it certainly was, with three miles of cakes . . . they came from all around the lakes, but they were thoroughbreds."

I appreciate the encomium, the lofty praise as "thoroughbreds." As late as 2013, the cavernous, decrepit machine shop of the Detroit Dry Dock Company, where the *Aurania*'s engine was built, remained. Today, only the east end wall of the facility is still with us. The Michigan Department of Natural Resources constructed a river interpretive center to it, connecting the old wall with its 1892 capstone, to future generations. The dry dock in which the *Aurania* and countless other lake boats were tended is also still there, albeit full of Detroit River water. You can visit both at the foot of Orleans Street. Whenever I do, I think of thoroughbreds.

Boneyard on the Detroit River

e can't pinpoint precisely where the bulk freighter *L. C. Waldo* was on the Detroit River at a quarter past 4 p.m. on the cool nineteenth day of August of 1907. The downbound ship was under the command of Captain John Duddleson, and in close vicinity and also bound down the river were the freighters *D. O. Mills*, brand new that season, and the *R. E. Schuck*. Upbound around the same time was the steamer *Saranac*.

It may be interesting to point out that six years into the future the *Waldo*, Duddleson still her commander, the *Mills*, and the *Schuck*, by that time renamed *Hydrus*, would all be victims of the Big Storm of 1913, the worst cyclone of widespread destruction and death ever to be witnessed on the Great Lakes. Whereas the crews of the *Mills* and the *Waldo* would survive, the *Hydrus* was lost with all hands; her wreck on the bottom of Lake Huron was not discovered until 2015. But such looking ahead is not the focus of this story. This is an account of boats and figures and memories that even in the faded past of the first decade of the twentieth century were things of the past.

Near the foot of Twenty Fourth Street in 1907—where today the nation's only floating zip code, the mailboat *J. W. Westcott II* docks—stood the Detroit Reduction Works. It was here that the offscourings of the city that hadn't found their way into

FIGURE 7. *Jay Cooke* early in her career. Courtesy of the Alpena County George N. Fletcher Library, Alpena, Michigan.

the river ended up for incineration. Daily, teams of horses clomped their wagon loads of trash to the facility. Municipalities were coming to grips with the pitfalls of urbanization as population expansion and consumerism sprouted the leftover waste of progress. The mephitic air over this section of Detroit could be smelled in any number of burgeoning American cities.

In this same location were a couple of relics from earlier times. Two derelict sidewheel steamers, the *Milton D. Ward* and the *City of Sandusky*, could be spotted through wafts of foul air. The *City of Sandusky* was once named *Jay Cooke*, and fondness for this veteran Detroit River passenger steamer ensured that, even with renaming, she would always sentimentally remain the *Cooke*. Nearly skeletal in her remaining frameworks and paddle boxes, her machinery removed, yet still afloat, she certainly brought memories to Duddleson. While his attention was probably on the careful navigation of the *Waldo* on the busy river and he was too busy to give the remains of the *Cooke* a long look, he must have known she was there. Way back in 1869, early in his lengthy sailing career on the lakes, he had been a wheelsman on the *Cooke*.

The vessel *Cooke* was a one-year-old in 1869, moving passengers and freight on the Detroit to Sandusky, Ohio, route. She followed on the heels of her predecessor sidewheel steamers *Philo Parsons* and the *Island Queen*. For many years, the *Cooke* was under the command of the affable Captain L. B. Goldsmith. The ship's sad remains could hardly bespeak the memories of fonder times. The *Cooke* made the run from Detroit to Sandusky in four hours and fifty minutes. Her numbers following the 1871 season tell the story of her quotidian work. She made 338 trips across Lake Erie, 32,000 miles, and in this year, without a single mishap. In late May of 1875, she carried forty-seven passengers on a fishing expedition, and the successful venture yielded a stunning account of fish populations in the lakes. On a single day, Monday, May 24, the fishermen reeled in 1,800 pounds of bass taken between Sandusky and the Lake Erie islands. The autumn of the same year, quite possibly with young Duddleson at the wheel, the *Cooke* was active in the movement of fresh produce harvested in the lakes' states. From Detroit she would run Michigan-grown apples and barley south and eastward and return with grapes from Ohio and Pennsylvania, along with other sundry cargoes.

Before exile to the boneyard, the *Cooke* had far less glamorous work. Stripped above her main deck, her lower works and engine also gone, the forlorn relic was engaged in running landfill material—dirt, gravel, stones, and even small rocks—from Detroit. One of her fill projects was carried out on marshy areas of Grosse Pointe, just above the mouth of the Detroit River.

An even younger Duddleson served as an Ohio volunteer in the Civil War, marching behind William Tecumseh Sherman on his slash-and-burn March to the Sea. As he climbed the ladder, leaving the wheel of the *Cooke* to successors, he became master of several ships before taking command of the *Waldo* in 1896. Including among them were the creatively named *F&PM No. 2*, *F&PM No. 3*, and *F&PM No. 4.*[*]

Back at the reduction works, the nearby *Ward* was outwardly more complete than the *Cooke*, although she had been charred by an earlier fire and her machinery had also been removed. Now an effete representative of passenger trade plying the Detroit River from the post–Civil War years until the close of the nineteenth century, her rotting timbers and forlorn sag belied more than twenty productive

---

[*]   F&PM were the initials of the Flint & Pere Marquette Railroad, to which the steamers belonged. They were registered with initials and numbers only. In 1901, the 2, 3, and 4 would be renamed *Pere Marquette*, followed by their number 2, 3, or 4.

and illustrious years of her paddle boxes thrashing the waters. When the *Ward* entered service in June of 1870, it was anticipated that she would be as speedy as the *Cooke*. A product of Marine City, Michigan, her original dimensions were roughly 167 feet in overall length, a beam of slightly over 28, and like many lake paddlers of the era, she had a rather shallow draft of seven-plus feet. Her first captain was M. S. Lathrup, and unlike the *Cooke* which traded on the route south from Detroit, the *Ward* worked north.

If not in her first years of service, by 1874, the *Ward* was operated by the Detroit-based Star Line. From the outset her route took her up Lake St. Clair and the St. Clair River to ports on the Michigan shore of Lake Huron. Prior to reaching them, her stops included Algonac, Marine City, St. Clair, Port Huron, and Sarnia, Ontario. Ports of call along Lake Huron were Lexington, Port Sanilac, Forestville, and White Rock, giving the *Ward* an aggressive agenda. The ship's popularity and success led to lengthening and improvements over the winter of 1874–1875 in Detroit. She was given an additional fifteen feet of length, stretching her out to 182 feet overall and expanding her gross rated tonnage to 544. In addition, the renovations gave her more sheer and a better looking stem, besides adding to her capacity, reported the *Detroit Free Press*. Her machinery was overhauled, decks improved along with the hull and cabins, and she was painted throughout. "She comes out fairly swelling with good looks and intentions," the laudatory *Detroit Free Press* summed things up. The refurbishments also earned her flagship honors for the Star Line.

The *Ward* occasionally offered a special day-long trip commencing at 9 a.m. from Detroit that included a couple of lengthy layovers. Captain P. Kenyon had charge of the steamer in this mid-to-late period of the 1870s. One stop on the day trip was the Star Island Lodge and Resort in the St. Clair Flats, where the *Ward* docked for more than six hours. Passengers could fish or rent small boats to further explore the delta or pursue idle pleasantries as fit their mood. Another two-and-a-half hours were spent at Marine City for dinner before the sidewheeler steamed north to Port Huron. After a brief docking, she headed home for Detroit, arriving at 9 p.m.

The ship's staple continued to be her runs up the Michigan thumb of Lake Huron. The *Ward* would eventually make the city of Port Austin, located at the tip of the thumb, her northernmost destination. Along the way she added ports of call at Sand Beach, Port Hope, and Grindstone City. In the summer of 1877, the *Ward* departed Detroit at 8 p.m. on Mondays, Wednesdays, and Fridays for what the *Detroit Free Press* would champion in its advertisement as "A Ride of 300 Miles." It cost five bucks round trip, meals and berth included. The ship returned to Detroit

FIGURE 8. Milton D. Ward in Detroit. Courtesy of the Alpena County George N. Fletcher Library, Alpena, Michigan.

a handful of hours before her next scheduled departure. Peering longer into the *Ward*'s past, we learn that in July of 1883 she would take on large quantities of wool at Port Austin, delivering it to Detroit, etching her name in the record as carrier of rare cargoes for a lake boat of any era.

Renovations to the *Ward* showered encomium on her in the spring of 1884, further testifying to the virtues and popularity of the ship. The April 15 edition of the *Detroit Free Press* reported as she was about to enter service that spring, "The artists have completed their work in the cabin of the steamer Milton D. Ward and have left her in truth, a floating gallery. The other workmen have nearly got through, nothing better left undone except the finishing touches in the bridal chamber." This leaves us with the takeaway that the elegant sidewheeler was a popular destination for nuptials. Or owners hoped it would be. Newspaper advertisements, broadcasting her schedule and destinations, called the *Ward* "staunch and commodious."

By the spring of 1886, the *Ward* was absorbed by the Cole-Grummond Line. Seemingly in remonstrance, her change of ownership was marked with mishaps. Principal owner-operator Stephen B. Grummond was a former mayor of Detroit. His efforts to retain political influence would one day have direct bearing not only on the direction of city business but also on the *Ward*. But first there was a rather costly collision on lake St. Clair for Grummond to deal with. Early in September of 1886, the *Ward* and a tiny, all-aft accommodated steam barge of a mere one-hundred-foot length, the *Norma*, came together. The *Norma* delivered the most serious damage in the encounter, landing the *Ward* in Detroit's Clark Dry Dock Company's yard for two weeks. Grummond hoped a cool thousand dollars would cover the cost of repairs; the necessary amount was triple that. When the ship returned to service, any vestige of the Cole-Grummond partnership was eliminated from her side—unrelated to the cost of repairs—and the "business card" on her bow now read, "Grummond's Line."

The *Ward*'s final transformation took place in 1888. Several staterooms were torn out to provide greater deck space, and her hurricane deck was extended. Her old pilothouse was replaced by a square unit, making her resemble her fleet mate, *Idlewild*. Four years later a set of circumstances involving the ship would ensnare both Stephen Grummond and his son, Ulysses Grant Grummond. It would play out in a lengthy, complex court battle replete with issues of immigration, infectious disease, maritime law, and insurance coverage liabilities.

Minutes taken from the public record of the Common Council of the City of Detroit and its health officials on August 30, 1892, addressed the growing concern of a cholera outbreak. Moreover, a wary finger was pointed at immigrants just arriving at the city. An unnamed official was later quoted as saying that "the only hope of keeping the city [safe] is in having a quarantine hospital built on a scow which we can keep in the stream." At the time, Stephen Grummond was a member of the board of health. Two weeks later, on September 14, upon selling the steamer to his son (who would later become the plaintiff in the legal ball of string), the elder man made an agreement for the sidewheeler to be requisitioned as a floating hospital for two years. The agreement explained that the boat would be used by the city as a hospital in which persons suspected of bringing germs of cholera from abroad could be isolated and cared for.

Cholera is a bacterial infection that is spread through contamination, usually in water supplies befouled by fecal matter. The first major outbreak in North America happened in 1832. At Detroit, deadly outbreaks occurred in 1834, 1849, 1856, and 1866, taking the lives of hundreds of residents. By the 1890s, major outbreaks in the United States had come to an end, but cases still popped up.

City Controller Black (no first name logged) announced that the boat could be secured for $5,000 for two years, while the city would be responsible for the $12,000 insurance premium to cover the same period. Grummond would see to it that the boat was caulked and put into shape, and with a wink and a nod, the former mayor informed the city, should they desire, could make an outright purchase following the term's expiration date. For $7,000, they could buy the *Ward*—less her engine. On November 22, the Common Council agreed to these conditions, and the *Ward*, however briefly, became a floating hospital on the Detroit River, just off the Water Works facility in the area of East Jefferson and Cadillac Streets. She was anchored close to shore, not midstream, where she could be boarded from land.

As might be imagined, many residents met the decision with concern and pushback. The dock space and gangplank to board the ship was in a residential section, and people living nearby felt threatened to possible exposure by the movements to-and-fro by the ship's staff. It's unclear how many patients were admitted aboard the *Ward*. Alarmed citizens' rose a powerful voice, and the Common Council brought an end to the quarantine ship shortly after approving it. For the players in the scheme, the episode would boil a pot of legal stew that wouldn't be resolved for years. A judgement was finally reached in a U.S. Court of Appeals in 1903.

By the summer of 1894, the Rileys, a husband-and-wife team, were ship keepers on the *Ward*. On August 17, while cooking dinner that evening, Mrs. Riley noticed smoke that was not coming from her stove. She hustled ashore and alerted employees of the Water Works, and they sent out the alarm. Shortly thereafter, the city's fire department engines 6, 7, and 13 responded, and so did their fireboat. The blaze had broken out at the *Ward*'s starboard wheel box and, although quickly extinguished, the water sprayed on the fire waterlogged her hull. The ship sank lower into the river, and her seriously charred hull painted a black eye on a once glorious countenance. Mrs. Riley pegged their losses of clothing, furniture, and silverware at $200.

The *Ward* sat in her dismal state and place for five years. The city Board of Public Works contracted with Luke Hawley to patch and pump out the ship and make her seaworthy for the short tow to the foot of Twenty-Fourth Street. The sad relic arrived on April 21, 1899. The city then began paying a nominal fee of ten bucks a month for decrepit dock space amid the foul aroma of the Reduction Plant.

Heading east, upriver above the dismal refuse center, there were at least two more decaying lake boats, timbers groaning as they faded to near obscurity. At the foot of East Grand Boulevard were the listing wooden-built steamer *H. B. Tuttle* and the barque *William Jones*. The *Tuttle*, an 1871 product of Cleveland, 159 feet in

FIGURE 9. *Milton D. Ward* at the "boneyard" on the Detroit River. Courtesy of the Alpena County George N. Fletcher Library, Alpena, Michigan, obtained through the Henry Ford Museum.

length, 552 tons, and last owned by a popular lakes' figure, C. E. Benham. Listing to starboard, the *Tuttle* appeared to be prow to prow with the *Jones*, which was listing to port. They seem to be pushed by some invisible force of nature, as if all of their battles with storms and the elements they endured on the lakes permanently heeled them over, even in the decayed stages of abandonment.

Most major Great Lakes ports, even minor ones, had a boneyard for abandoned vessels, particularly in the wooden-boat era. Worn out, stripped of anything of value, the hulks rotted away on river and lakefronts. Usually, the waterfronts where they rested were city owned or of no commercial value. Once enrollment documents were surrendered, or closed, so too were legal responsibilities. We can think of them as an abandoned vehicle on a sideroad with the vehicle identification number removed.

When a photograph of the two appeared in the *Detroit Free Press* in the June 7, 1908, edition, the newspaper account mentions C. A. Chamberlain, presumably a Detroiter. Chamberlain was in possession of a precious keepsake from the *Jones*, a leather-bound Bible, inscribed in gilt letters, presented by "the Cleveland Bible Society to the barque William James." When the *Jones* was built at Black River (Lorain), Ohio, in 1862, it was named for the owner. Inside the bible, on the "family records" page for notations, there were two telling entries:

A. P. Anderson, seaman, fell overboard in the St. Clair rapids and drowned, November 15, 1866.

John O'Grady, seaman, fell overboard 40 miles S.W. by W from Long Point, Lake Erie, and drowned August 26, 1900, about age 19.

Not to disparage words in the Bible, but there is no "St. Clair rapids." One thing you will find as you research Great Lakes maritime history in the nineteenth century is that there were alarming numbers of sailors that drowned falling overboard. Untold numbers of them never had their names reported in a newspaper, let alone inscribed in a Bible.

Life jackets, life preservers—both, personal floatation devices—date to the 1850s. Whether worn or a floating ring tossed from a ship, they were constructed of cork. The effectiveness of the latter, assuming one was nearby to be thrown when a sailor was lost overboard, was minimal at best. Many of the unfortunate sailors that went overboard never surfaced. It was rare when bodies were recovered.

When I researched the dates surrounding the deaths of Anderson and O'Grady, I came up empty, save an account from the *Detroit Free Press* in the November 18, 1866, edition, three days after Anderson's demise. Mid-lake, Lake Michigan, off Grand Haven, Michigan, the steamer *Detroit* reported sighting a "fore-and-aft" rigged lumber vessel, waterlogged and deserted. Featuring a lead-colored hull with white rails, her mainmast was ripped free and hanging at her side, the foretopmast and jibboom gone, and listing to such a degree that her opposite rail was submerged below the lake surface. "The vessel is without a doubt the Wm. Jones of Chicago," the report emphatically stated. Maybe it was, but the fore-and-aft description allows for some doubt, as the *Jones* was barque rigged, thus the error, if one was extant, may have been in describing the ship's rigging. It's also possible the *Jones* was by then rigged as a fore-and-aft schooner, an updating of barque origins from since launching, not an unusual practice on lake boats.

The sight of the derelict *Jones* and *Tuttle*, following the corpses of the *Ward* and *Cooke* would be plenty of fodder to cause one to contemplate days gone by and benchmarks of lakes' history. Still ahead, working your way up the river, near the foot of Belle Isle were two more disabled monuments to the Great Lakes' shipping past, half-submerged and utterly broken, as if casualties from a naval battle at sea. One was the nearly submerged *Montpelier*, her weather-beaten masts, still standing, making a defiant protest to her pitiful condition. It was her nearby companion that, besides showing a thread more resilience to old age and decades of sailing long behind her, crowned these boneyard recollections. It was the defiant and gallant barque *Maria Martin*. A name sweet and lilting, befitting a homecoming queen, the *Martin* was a long-forgotten lake boat that has a historic record deep and colorful as is her name eupeptic.

The *Martin* was launched on April 14, 1866, from Cleveland. It was launched the same day as another Cleveland product destined for a long sailing career on the Great Lakes, the *Goshawk*. *Goshawk* was a creation of the Lafriniere shipyard and the *Martin* of the famed and fruitful Quayle & Martin yard. The *Martin* was named after John Martin's daughter; he, the Martin partner in the prolific shipbuilding duo. Both ships were similar in size; the *Martin* grossed 568 tons, the *Goshawk* slightly less. Overall dimensions for the *Martin* have eluded my search, but by comparing tonnage numbers, we can arrive at safely guessing the ship was close to the *Goshawk*'s: 185 feet in overall length, a beam of thirty-one, and drawing twelve feet of water.

The *Martin* would immediately commence laying the foundation of her remarkable career on the lakes. At the wee hours of 2 a.m., June 22, 1866, on the southern end of the Detroit River near Bar Point, the *Martin* was downbound in tow of the tug *McClellan*. Upbound was the Northern Transportation Company's propeller *Cleveland*, bound for Chicago from Ogdensburg, New York. Passing signals were exchanged, yet inexplicably the *Martin* rumbled into the *Cleveland* on her port side between numbers 4 and 5 staterooms. So deep did the *Martin*'s cutwater penetrate the propeller that in a matter of a mere ten minutes the *Cleveland* was on the bottom.

All sixty of the *Cleveland*'s passengers were awakened by the loud, shattering impact. Some were momentarily trapped by fallen timbers and injured by splintered beams, and all were stunned, bewildered, and sleepy, in various states of dishabille. Miraculously, no lives were lost, and this fortunate turn of events could be attributed to the *Martin* being drawn alongside the sinking *Cleveland*, so that everyone, passengers and crew alike, could scramble aboard the assailant barque. In most cases, everyone lost virtually everything except what they were wearing. One of three New Yorkers occupying stateroom number 2, Harley Parker, lost a span of trotting horses bound for Chicago, valued at a significant amount of money—$3,000.

In late October 1870, the *Martin*, under command of Captain Burke (no first name recorded) had departed Escanaba, Michigan, with a cargo of iron ore destined for an undisclosed port. In miserable weather, with winds reaching gale strength, the *Martin* ran aground in shoal water off Whiskey Island in northern Lake Michigan. We can determine two things about the *Martin* in this precarious state: one, she sported a black hull color, at least for a while in her career; two, she was an unmitigated mess. She was evacuated. Burke caught a ride on the propeller *Idaho* to Detroit where he sought to secure a wrecking tug. On October 29, four days after the *Martin* ran afoul, she was stripped and abandoned to the insurance underwriters. Burke was undeterred. On Halloween day, he contracted with the famous wrecker *Leviathan* to release and secure the *Martin*, "terms, $5,000 or nothing."

Harsh weather vexed the salvage work. On November 16, the *Leviathan* succeeded in towing the broken *Martin* to the Campbell, Owen & Company dry dock at Detroit. The diagnosis here tells us even more about the durability of the ship and the owner's faith in her. Her hull was broken in four places. Yet some familiar with her believed she could transcend a fracture that would have doomed most boats, and over the winter they set about mending her.

Conducting extensive research into Great Lakes vessel histories is much like excavating an archaeological grid. Newspaper microfilm serves as the screening mesh enabling a researcher to bring to light once-hidden "artifacts." The incidents unearthed are gathered like flint points or uniform buttons or coinage, and the stories they reveal in turn enable the researcher/writer to become the raconteur. Accepting this analogy, the late spring of 1876 provides us with information about the *Martin* we could hardly conceive.

The winter of 1875–1876 on the upper Great Lakes was savage. The hyperborean ice conditions extended through the late spring of 1876, and well into the month of June. One of a small group of boats marooned in ice off Duluth was the *Martin*. The boat had been locked up by ice for an extended period, and the crew resorted to living on half rations as the food supply dwindled. To their good fortune, the Canadian propeller *Quebec* was also held captive nearby, and its crew provided meals for the hungry *Martin* crewmen. The men had genuinely feared starvation until the Canadians intervened. The rigorous, unrelenting icy situation at Duluth inspired the *Detroit Tribune* to editorialize in its June 6 edition:

A telegram from Duluth of Saturday last reported the Str. Fremont and one or two other boats ice-bound at Duluth. It appears that the northeast wind has driven ice, of which there remains immense fields, to the head of Lake Superior, blocking up the port of Duluth. The ice is said to extend out ten miles or more.

We suggest that the citizens of Duluth advertise a great centennial skating carnival for the next Fourth of July upon the ice of the harbor. It would attract more visitors than any other entertainment that could be afforded.

Between bouts of tribulations the *Martin* was sailed by at least two noteworthy and toweringly courageous men. Andrew Kelly served as the ship's first mate in 1877. His storied career was already well developed by the time he sailed the ship. He and five others were strong enough to swim ashore on November 14, 1871, when the schooner *Resolute* wrecked off Long Point in Lake Erie, a disaster in which two, including the ship's female cook, died of exposure, fearful of leaving the stranded ship. He later sailed on another vessel lost by collision on the same lake, the *Charles K. Nimms.* Years after that, he and fellow crew members would save a crew of seven from a sinking lumber scow, yet again on Lake Erie.

Another former first mate from the *Martin*, who would go on to earn his captain's papers and sail the ship in that capacity as well, a man earning a giant reputation in a remarkably adventurous career, was Charles W. Lockwood. A native of Ashtabula, Ohio, Lockwood studied and worked at his sailing career during an eight-month voyage on the sailing ship *Hemisphere*, San Francisco to Hong Kong. His ocean-going experiences would later take him to various Mediterranean port cities, and he also sailed between Boston and Philadelphia and New Orleans. There is testimony to his character when in 1868, in command of the Boston-based *Ward J. Parks*, bound for a Mediterranean port with an extraordinarily valuable cargo of raisins—price tagged at nearly a quarter of a million dollars—a smallpox outbreak decimated the crew. Lockwood scarcely turned in, once manning the helm for fourteen straight hours during especially heavy weather.

More costly repairs had to be made on the *Martin* in June of 1884. On the ninth, she collided with the schooner *Emma C. Hutchinson* off Milwaukee and sustained heavy damage. Her mizzen topmast, mainsail, yawl, and davits were lost. When the topmast fell to the deck, it smashed several deck beams and planking abaft her main hatch.

Here and there, throughout the roomy halls of Great Lakes' history, we find incidents of boats sinking at docks. Indecorous, but much preferred to foundering in

FIGURE 10. *Maria Martin* in Chicago, 1884. Courtesy of the Alpena County George N. Fletcher Library, Alpena, Michigan.

the depths of the lakes. On May 14, 1886, coal-laden at a dock at Racine, Wisconsin, the *Martin* suffered this humiliation when she sprung a leak. The brief describing the incident in the *Detroit Free Press* succinctly read, "Her three pumps wouldn't keep her afloat and she sank."

Of the protagonists addressed in this riverscape boneyard collective, most were in their final resting place. Their crumbling remains would finally fall apart and sink into oblivion or be covered over by fill projects. The *Ward* and *Cooke* never moved again. Nor, as near as can be determined, did the *Tuttle* or *Jones*. This would not be the case for the *Martin*. The last photo taken of her, which appeared in the May 21, 1908, edition of the *Detroit Free Press*, illustrated the *Martin*'s sad state, but it wasn't the end of her. The remains of the *Montpelier* are shown in the same photo, and it's an even sorrier sight. Notwithstanding, the *Martin*'s bowsprit is gone. A lone mast protrudes from her drooping deck, and even at that it is not fully intact. The *Detroit Free Press* wrote the forlorn barque was, "like an old, blind horse, humanely turned out to pasture." She was then owned by a Detroiter, Captain John Dorrington, and his affection for the *Martin* was evident, but government intervention forced his hand.

Dorrington spent summer months aboard the *Martin*, despite her dilapidated condition. He romanticized the ship and vessels of her era, saying, "They are like veteran soldiers and ought to be guarded." He also allowed her weary, beaten hull to serve as a floating billboard, as advertisement for local clothiers were pasted to her sides. Highly unusual, but the U.S. Army Corps of Engineers were not impressed with the signage, and since the boat had no lights, they deemed the *Martin* a menace to navigation. After legal challenges fighting the corps' decision to the extent of his abilities, or perhaps his wallet's, Dorrington finally gave up the ship. On June 17, 1910, the *Martin* was towed to Amherstburg, Ontario, by her new owner, David Hackett. Hackett earned $400 from the city of Detroit for the job, along with ownership of the *Martin.* Obstreperous to the finish, Dorrington claimed the government [city] wasted $400 of the people's money to pump out the ship before it was towed from the foot of Belle Isle; he said he could have done it for twenty-five bucks. The illustrious *Martin* ultimately disintegrated at Amherstburg.

In our current time, when low water levels persist in areas of the Great Lakes and river basins, relics of lake boats forgotten in unsuspected boneyards can emerge into view. At Grand Haven, Michigan, on Harbor Island, the remains of the *L. L. Barth* and the *Aurora* were visible as late as 2012. On the Saginaw River at West Bay City, Michigan, at the site of the once-prolific Davidson Shipbuilding Company, the ribs of several lake boat skeletons may be visible, including those of the *Sacramento*, once one of the largest wooden-built steamships to ply the lakes. These ships may not have been freighted with adventures like the *Martin* was, but when water levels allow us to catch sight of these historic remnants, they can shoulder the memories of the *Ward* and *Jones* and carry them.

Harry Coulby's Gruesome Gift

By 1910, Harry Coulby's omnipresence was felt everywhere in the realm of Great Lakes shipping. With his powerful influence and skills, he managed the affairs of the Pickands Mather fleet of boats. Simultaneously, he called the shots of the enormous Pittsburgh Steamship Company vessels. He accomplished this feat from an upper floor of Cleveland's Western Reserve Building, not far from the Cuyahoga River.

His workday entailed all aspects of communications vital to business: messages sent and received, notes and letters addressed, and phone calls answered and made, as the telephone's popularity expanded. There were business documents, registered letters, parcels, and assorted packages crossing his desk, all quotidian business operations.

On July 1 of the same year, he opened a package, the contents of which shocked him. It may very well have, in the chilling moments of revelation, even given him pause about his relocation to Cleveland and his ascent to power in the shipping scene. Inside the package was a jar, and inside the jar was a severed human ear. Stunned and appalled in his tightly organized office, he could never have imagined such a scene playing out in any chapter of his remarkable story.

Born in Claypole, Lincolnshire, Great Britain, in 1863, Coulby spent his restless youth nearer Sherwood Forest than the North Sea. The pedantic young Coulby was interested in seafaring and geography at a tender age, wistfully pining for waters far from his realm: the Great Lakes. It is curious how a youth fascinated with the maritime world, coming from one of the world's profound seafaring nations, dreamed of the distant lakes of North America. Years later he would profess, "The name itself, 'Great Lakes,' fascinates me. I wanted to see those lakes. If possible, I was going to sail them."

Industrious and autodidactic, Coulby embarked upon adventure and untethered journeys that one day would deliver him to his freshwater paradise. In the journey getting there, his biography was filled with remarkable experiences, combined with indefatigable drive. He worked to gain experience non-remuneratively, spending countless hours to better his lot by learning to read telegraph code, and thus, deciphering its language. Ultimately it paid off. He took a job with a cable company, based in Santiago, Cuba, when the offer arose.

Accenting Coulby's personal odyssey were the effects of landing in tropical Cuba. Shortly after arriving he contracted malaria. Combined with issues of his salary, his compromised physical condition drove him to the desperation of his next decision: he stowed away on a steamship bound for New York.

When he arrived at Cleveland in 1884, Coulby reached his personal nirvana. The sweet, fresh water of the Great Lakes, the pursuit of his childhood romance, were now at his feet. His drive, work ethic, and boundless energy saw to it he built his own stage. The fire for business acumen he possessed grew into a raging inferno of success on the shores of Lake Erie. Upon mastering a new device known as the typewriter and currying favor with men impressed with his vigor and drive, Coulby and his clerical skills landed him employment with Pickands Mather. Iron-ore mines, ships, and, most of all, those unparalleled Great Lakes were now his world. In looking back at his fortunes later, Coulby would say, "A chance is enough for anybody, especially in the United States in the twentieth century, when opportunities for young men are better than at any time since Christopher Columbus set foot on America." Forgiving Coulby his gaffe of historical inaccuracy and his privilege as a white male living at a perceived time of unequaled opportunity, he certainly grabbed the brass ring of prosperity through hard work and enterprise.

Coulby's diligence and drive propelled him from clerical work to managing the expanding Pickands Mather fleet of ore boats in only a few years. A meteoric rise that wouldn't end with this accomplishment, even as the company absorbed vessels from outside fleets into their stable under his direction. When the monolithic U.S. Steel Company was formed early in 1901, and their Pittsburgh Steamship Company's marine division became the largest fleet on the Great Lakes, it was beset by gremlins of bad management, scheduling nightmares, and sundry maritime accidents. One of U.S. Steel's co-founders, Elbert H. Gary—former corporate lawyer, judge, and namesake of the industrial rakehell Indiana Lake Michigan port city—approached Coulby in 1904. Gary was mindful of Coulby's success managing the expanding fleet of Pickands Mather boats and wanted him to take over management of the Pittsburgh fleet as well. After reaching an agreement that Coulby could retain his partnership with Pickands Mather, he agreed to take on the task. Now managing two storied colossuses, it was the only time in Great Lakes history such a threshold was achieved.

Comments, remarks, and reports about the martinet Coulby referred to him as a "czar" or "master" of the lakes. Regardless the affectation, Coulby was versed and adroit at every aspect of lakes shipping. Physically, he bore a strong resemblance to the American film and television actor Pat Hingle. Hingle's portrayal of Thomas Edison in General Electric promotions brought Edison to life. Coulby's mansion at Wickliffe, Ohio, serves at the municipality's city hall today.

His accomplishments not replicated, his efficiencies unsurpassed, his standing in the historic rolls of lakes' lore unreachable, Harry Coulby loathed labor unions. This loathing was epidemic among the powerbrokers of powerful corporate trusts, all contemptuous of organized labor. These were incendiary times in the American labor movement as workers fought back against the monolithic bastions of industry in the early twentieth century. Coulby would do whatever it took, even if it meant throwing money at hot spots to ameliorate labor tensions. Even if only a temporary fix, whatever it took to keep labor unions chained and toothless.

In these contentious times, the hideous parcel landed on Coulby's desk. The ghoulish package had been mailed from Buffalo, and authorities knew the identity of the now one-eared man: Edward Frazer. Poor Frazer would most likely have been written off as an unfortunate victim of a heinous, deranged crime, quite possibly forgotten, had his ear ended up anywhere else than a jar now in the hands of the most celebrated and influential man on the Great Lakes. Of course, the only reason he was holding it was for the very same reasons of power and influence. Luckless Frazer was a non-union sailor. In the evil, convoluted reasoning of the men who mugged Frazer and the sick villain that slashed off his ear, sending it to Coulby would ensure that their voices of unionism and defiance against the trusts be heard, while sending the message that no dark tactic was below their dastardliness.

The value of poor Frazer's ear, hardly worth digging into before being mailed to such an important figure, suddenly turned the incident into the Lindberg baby case. The Buffalo Police Department accelerated their investigation. Post office inspectors soon joined the action to solve the brutal crime.

On July 13, in a crowded courtroom in Buffalo, four men suspected in the case were released on their own recognizance as the charges against them fell apart. The *Detroit Free Press*, in exasperation after there was no evidence to charge the four, wrote, "After repeating day after day since their arrest the mystery of Frazer's ear had been solved." By mid-month, Frazer himself made a simple, humane, if not futile request, for what, at best, could be a worthless outcome: he wanted his detached ear returned to him.

One of the early suspects in the case, Michael Courtney, was arrested a few days after being exonerated in the ear case. Ironically, it was for assaulting a sailor. That too happened in Buffalo, on the corner of Main and Lloyd Streets. His only explanation was that he was drunk. His action cost him twenty-five days in jail, and rekindled suspicions of his possible guilt in the ear-cutting travesty.

The diligence of the Buffalo Police Department finally paid dividends. In September, three men were bound over for examination in the case. Courtney was not among them. At their trial in November, one of the men, Joseph Myers, aka Mike Armstrong, was found guilty of the detestable crime. His sentence was severe—six to thirteen-and-a-half years. To be served at New York's redoubtable hellhole, Auburn Prison, where the nation's first execution by electric chair was held.

The bon vivant Coulby smoked fine cigars and could spin long yarns, so it seems fair to wonder if the horrible surprise of being sent Frazer's ear was a story he recounted occasionally between measured puffs. Likewise, it seems fair to wonder if Frazer's ear was ever returned to him.

Through the Wheelhouse Windows of the *N. J. Nessen*

O n the odious night of October 22, 1929, the wooden-built steamer *N. J. Nessen* was not only feeling its age, but it was also fighting for its life. Bound for Cleveland from Detroit with a ferrous, ignoble cargo of scrap steel in its hold and in its fiftieth season, the *Nessen* was ancient. Roughed up by rogue, white-capped, jade-green Lake Erie seas, Captain Bernard Benson could only hope that his ship could endure yet another bout of foul weather the lakes could dish out. Peering out the wheelhouse windows into darkness settled over the roiling lake, he knew the *Nessen* was likely to meet its fate somewhere along the Canadian shoreline.

I thought of Benson and the *Nessen*'s dilemma gazing through the pilothouse windows of the car ferry *City of Milwaukee.* The car ferry's existence bears a direct connection to the storm Benson's steamer was battling. The car ferry *City of Milwaukee,* a historic landmark and sentinel on Manistee Lake, doubles as a floating museum and berth and breakfast. It is a must-see and sleep-over for any lover of Great Lakes marine lore and unique vessels to sail its waters. It remains, ninety-one years after entry into service, a period correct portal into the era of the Great Depression through its magnificent marine architecture. Almost nothing has changed. Walking through the salon between the forward observation room and the galley aft, its impressive appointments are still intact. This corridor of staterooms, finished in rich oak and artistic touches, belies the unglamorous work the ship was built for: ferrying railroad cars across Lake Michigan. Although the *City of Milwaukee* will likely forever call Manistee, Michigan, home, it never operated in the cross-lake service from the port.

When the boat came out in January of 1931, a product of the Manitowoc Shipbuilding Company, it was the sixth and final of its style. This included two sister ships—the *Madison* and *Grand Rapids*—two more sailing for the Pere Marquette Railroad line, and one working for the Ann Arbor Railroad. These car ferries ride high out of the water, their towering sides necessary to accommodate the railroad cars carried in their cavernous holds. The *City of Milwaukee*, like the others whose design she replicated, could carry thirty cars on four sets of tracks. Her look of today—sporting twin fore-and-aft smokestacks—striped, red, white, and blue over her white-topped black hull give her appealing visuals. George W. Hilton, in his epic treatise on these resourceful crafts, *The Great Lakes Car Ferries*, summed it up reverently. "In addition, these ships probably represented the aesthetic peak of car ferry design. . . . However, all art is properly judged relative to the limitations of the art form, and within the restrictions imposed by the requirements of a car ferry, these six ships as they were built were handsomely proportioned, majestic and impressive."

The *City of Milwaukee*'s entered service—first between Grand Haven, Michigan, and Milwaukee, and in 1933, when the Grand Trunk Line moved its eastern terminus, to Muskegon from that point on—was clouded in the dark recesses of the Great Depression. The dire economic times were compounded by the tenebrous occasion for the car ferry's construction: it was built to replace a lost ferry from the fleet. The ship, the *Milwaukee*, disappeared on Lake Michigan claiming all-hands, perhaps fifty souls in all, on October 22, 1929.

The tragedy of the *Milwaukee* loss revealed the audacious personality of her captain, Robert McKay, cementing the legacy of his sobriquet, "Bad Weather." It is a story of heartbroken survivors, as in the case of two young boys. When they heard that two bodies from the ship had been recovered, they went into the Grand Haven office of the Grand Trunk terminal. Curious officials wanted to know why they were interested in the grim news, and they responded because their father was on the boat. The sad loss told of the transient make up of crews sailing not only car ferries but also all vessels working the lakes at the time. In the case of the *Milwaukee*, some of the victim's names and hometowns were never recorded, and among the lost were men identified simply as "Bozo" and "Big Bozo," "Long" Martin and "Kid" Moran.

There was joie de vivre for several of the car ferry's crewmen. Harry Moss was aboard ship that fateful day. He was sent into town to deliver a message, and it turned into an errand of mercy. The *Milwaukee* had sailed by the time he returned to the dock. Second mate Helmer Malm took a brief hiatus and was married three days before, resulting in perhaps the sweetest honeymoon ever. Steve Wakonewski and Carl Sjohim believed not even Bad Weather McKay would sail, so they never bothered showing up at the dock. "We would have gone along, but we didn't think the ship was going," Wakonewski said. "We heard everything else was getting under cover. It was kind of tough when we figured our jobs might be gone, but I guess it's alright now," he told a reporter from the *Milwaukee Sentinel* three days after the boat sank. The *City of Milwaukee* was affixed with the "City of" in her name to distinguish her from the lost *Milwaukee.*

Roaming the *City of Milwaukee*'s riveted, steel-plated decks, I was reminded of James Burke's marvelous BBC series from years ago, *Connections.* Part artifice, part historical documentary, Burke fashions a lustrous mosaic pieced together by connecting seemingly unrelated places, incidents, and figures from the past into standards of modernity. Looking out through the big car ferry's pilothouse windows, I was overtaken with thoughts of the *Milwaukee.* Through those windows, I imagined connections of lakes' history during those wild howling weather days of late October 1929. The foul weather was protracted and far-reaching. On the night the *Milwaukee* disappeared from Lake Michigan, destiny was playing its hand on the *Nessen.* What culminated later in this saga underpins the connections of stories of lake boat episodes worthy of Burke's approval.

When the boat entered service in the summer of 1880, the name *Nessen* was years into her future. A product of Black River (Lorain), Ohio, shipbuilder Henry Root, the vessel was christened *H. Luella Worthington.* Even in this nascent stage, the boat had established a profound connection. When launched, she was comprised of recycled components—engine, boiler, smokestack, shaft, and a single nine-foot propeller. Those cannibalized parts were salvaged from a villainously famous ship, the *Meteor.* The tarnished reputation of the *Meteor* was pinned to the tragic collision with her fleet sister, the *Pewabic.* On August 9, 1865, the *Meteor* rammed the *Pewabic* on Lake Huron, some six miles from Thunder Bay Island. The *Pewabic* was mortally holed and sank quickly in 150 feet of water, claiming the lives of well over one hundred people, perhaps as many as 125. Survivors were rescued by the *Meteor.*

The *Worthington*, named after the wife of the ship's owner, George Worthington, was otherwise new in every respect. It was average size for its time, 148 feet in length, registering 440 gross tons. According to notes in the Runge file of the Milwaukee Public Library's fine holdings, the boat had three eight-by-twelve-foot hatches. Worthington was proprietor of a grindstone business based in Cleveland, and from this central location, he would ship stones nationwide. The stones were loaded aboard ships at Grindstone City, Michigan, on Lake Huron, and overtly it was for this purpose the ship was built. Worthington had years of interests and connections to shipping on the Great Lakes and beyond. It was clear from the outset that his boat wouldn't be confined to merely the movement of stones, and many cargoes would make up her payloads. The Worthingtons were aboard when the ship made its maiden voyage on July 26, 1880.

By 1883 the *Worthington* was towing the schooner, *Shawnee*. It was widespread practice on the lakes as tandems could greatly increase, often doubling, payloads. Marine news columns reported the movements of ships daily and provided insight into their activities. Additionally, it gave us indications of Worthington's savvy skills in procuring cargoes. One sterling example comes from May of that year. He negotiated rates for the duo before it left Cleveland. When the boats reached Toledo, they were loaded with coal for Marquette, Michigan, at seventy-five cents a ton. Returning to the lower lakes with iron ore, he had them locked in at a $1.15 per ton. This business acumen would be evident throughout Worthington's ownership. Another example of his willingness to haul wild cargoes came the following year. In June, they unloaded coal at Buffalo from Detroit and returned with barrel staves, hogsheads, and pipes. Barreled salt cargoes were frequently rolled aboard the ship for delivery to various ports.

The engine from the *Meteor* was worn out. It was twenty years old in 1884 and perhaps additionally stressed by the fire which claimed the rest of the ship in 1873, making an upgrade necessary. Over the winter of 1884–1885, in Cleveland, the *Worthington* was repowered. A fore-and-aft compound engine with cylinders nineteen and thirty-six inches by a thirty-inch stroke, manufactured by the firm of Wilson & Hendrie of Montague, Michigan, was installed. Once ready for service in the spring of 1885, the boat was once again paired with the *Shawnee*.

The following year even more changes came. Deck work was done this time, and the alterations were not directed by Worthington: He sold his wife's namesake to Spaulding & Company of Chicago. At their behest, the conversions were made to employ the ship in the lumber trade, running her between Green Bay and Chicago.

The *Worthington* parted ways with her old running mate *Shawnee*. Spaulding & Company would retain her name, and she was paired with two schooner/barges for tow, the *Jones* and the *John B. Wilbur.*

On May 9, 1889, the *Worthington* was plodding along on the Chicago River, approaching the Rush Street Bridge. An engine malfunction prevented the boat from responding to her wheelhouse command, and she plowed into the bridge, shearing off the roof of her pilothouse, fore rigging, stays, and foremast. It appears to be the first serious accident suffered by the boat.

Eleven years later, again on the Chicago River, the *Worthington* was the protagonist in a novel episode of maritime misadventure. She was outbound on July 9 when a fire broke out in her aft cabin near the smokestack. Her crew hastily went into their fire muster, and her captain steered the ship up to the conveniently nearby Chicago Fire Department fireboat, *Illinois.*[*] Certainly this wowed the docked fireboat's crew: a fire coming to them. The *Worthington*'s crew displayed coolness and dexterity, connecting their water hose to above-deck tanks, playing it on the flames. In tandem with the *Illinois*, the fire was quickly extinguished.

The headiness of the *Worthington*'s crew may not be specifically linked to an incident from two years prior; nonetheless, it is an interesting and informative chapter in the ship's career involving water tanks and potable water. In 1898, the *Worthington*'s chief engineer, H. F. Otto, was a patient at the Marine Hospital in Chicago. It was uncertain what caused his hospitalization, but it was strongly suspected it was water—believed to be potable—from the *Worthington*'s above-deck water tanks used for drinking and cooking. Dr. Henry Sawtelle, a staff surgeon at the hospital, questioned Otto about the freshwater supply aboard ship. Sawtelle hoped to learn if tainted drinking water may have been the culprit. He was also anxious to learn if it was possible that the toxic water of the Chicago River had been admitted into the *Worthington*'s wholesome water supply. Otto later penned a letter in response.

He described the function of suction apparatus employed on vessels he was aware of. Pipes from two to five inches in diameter, with pumps usually housed

---

[*]   As this is written in the spring of 2022, and "connections" is the theme of this chapter, the *Illinois* is still with us, but not as a fireboat. In 1941, it was repowered with a diesel engine, converted to a tugboat, and renamed *John Roen III*. In 1974, it was again renamed *John M. Selvick*. Retired in 2015, it is currently lying at the yard of the Calumet River Fleeting and Chicago Dry Dock on the Calumet River in South Chicago, awaiting what appears will be an imminent date with the scrapper's torch.

FIGURE 11. *N. J. Nessen* photo op long before mandatory load lines on lake boats. Courtesy of the Alpena County George N. Fletcher Library, Alpena, Michigan.

in the engine room, would be alongside the ship with the suction head below the water surface. With the pipes below the water line, and thus, always full, there was potential for hazard. He wrote to Sawtelle, "A steamer lying in the Chicago River for several days will naturally have her suction pipes filled with Chicago River water, and unless extra precautions are taken to withdraw this water, it will be pumped into the tanks when said tanks are being filled with Lake Michigan water."

Otto broke it down, as only an engineer could, how much water a three-inch diameter pipe, ten feet long, holds in gallons, down to ten-thousandths of an ounce, and how dangerous even the slightest amount of Chicago River water could be to the health of a crew should it make its way into the drinking water tanks. He informs us of even more about the *Worthington*, continuing, "on [the] steamer on which I am employed a discharge from [the] pump, whereby I am able to clean pipes thoroughly from all impure water before filling tanks, and all steam vessels should have [the] same or better arrangements." Although Otto's letter to Sawtelle invites questions, it also sheds light on the quotidian use of untreated water collected on Lake Michigan for drinking water.

In 1903 the *Worthington* was sold to John O. Nessen, a lumberman with connections in both Chicago and Manistee. The boat was renamed *N. J. Nessen*, in honor
of Nessen's son, Newel John. The following spring, the boat's first mate, Martin
Peterson, and first mate of a fleet sister, Eugene Hibberdine of the *F. W. Fletcher*,
unwillingly found themselves in the center of controversy and legal machinations
of competing labor organizations and their respective directives.

Following their first trip of the season, when it was announced the prevailing
wages were to be pared back, they refused to return to their posts. The stance was
urged and supported by the Masters and Pilots Association, to which they both
belonged. The Lumber Carriers Association, along with the *Nessen*'s owner, and to
which contracts the boat was bound, directed them to return to duty. Both sides dug
in and held their ground, and for several days, there was no progress. Ultimately it
was punted to the Lake Carriers' Association, the overarching organization presided
over by William Livingstone, one of the most powerful figures in the businesses of
Great Lakes commerce. Livingstone called a summit, and the chess match between
these competing sides played out at Detroit's Hotel Normandie.

When resolved, the rate of pay to mates remained the same, and the first two
lumber boats to steam back to work were the *Nessen* and the *Fletcher*. In the arena
of union unrest this spring, wages for ship captains were also on the chopping
block. They reacted to this insult by leaving their ships at the docks. Eventually the
backlash from the strike would sting them too like a scorpion's tail when they lost
the dispute, changing the landscape of unionism on lake boats for years to come.

On April 10, 1907, pitching a plume of coal smoke and muscling her way through
ice on Pine Lake (Lake Charlevoix) in the scenic "little finger" area of Michigan's
lower peninsula, the *Nessen*'s Captain Edwardson was heading her for the open
waters of Lake Michigan. Two weeks earlier, Edwardson sailed the *Nessen* into
Michigan City, Indiana, with a load of lumber. A March delivery was the earliest in
the port's history to receive a lumber shipment. The boat had just loaded lumber
at the East Jordan, Michigan. About a mile above Ironton, the ice found a weak gap
in the ship's planking and opened her hull like a steamed mussel. In a matter of
minutes, the *Nessen* was on the bottom in twenty feet of water.

The Nessen Lumber Company dispatched the *Fletcher* to the scene and relieved
the submerged *Nessen* of her lumber cargo. They also sent diver Frank Hughes to the
site to access the predicament. Hughes's finding was grim. The planking in the ship's
stem, just back of the sheathing over her hull, had opened wide enough for a man to
pass through. Raising the boat was going to require considerable effort. Canvas was

FIGURE 12. *Nessen* sunk on Pine Lake; fleet sister, *Fletcher*, standing by. Courtesy of the William Lafferty Collection.

used to cover the holes, then, almost mummy-like, and an eight-foot-wide strip of heavy canvas, three hundred feet in length, was passed around the hull and nailed in place. Salvage crews worked on raising the ship for ten days. When pumps were put aboard and activated, the *Nessen* responded like a mylar balloon given a boost of helium and was quickly afloat.

On the fateful night of October 22, 1929, Benson probably wasn't thinking of the incident on Pine Lake in his aged ship's past. Most likely he was hoping to keep the ship from finding another lake bottom. As the *Nessen* was fighting for survival on roiling, wicked Lake Erie, at Port Huron, Michigan, some fifty vessels were riding at anchor, either in lower Lake Huron or in the St. Clair River to avoid the furious weather. The extended range of this fierce weather system covered much of Lake Superior as well. There are photographs of casualties of the blow to exemplify the drama of the storm they endured. The *James E. Davidson*, a 524-foot, steel-hulled ore boat under command of Captain Herman Winkler, was one of the boats savaged in the storm. The ship had her anchors snapped from the pockets, railings were torn off, and hatch covers were damaged. When the *Davidson* reached Fort William, Ontario, on the twenty-fourth, a photographer captured her image. Most alarming was the sight of her Texas deck, stove in like a canned good fallen to the floor. Meanwhile, on the same lake, the Great Lakes Transit Company's veteran package freighter, *Chicago*, came to grief on Michipicoten Island. The ship, Captain P. J. Farrell at the helm, gouged her bottom away on rocks studding the island's shore. It perched at a precarious angle to port, the bow was much higher than the submerged stern. This striking predicament, too, was captured on film. None too soon. Shortly thereafter, the *Chicago* lost this tenuous grip on the outcropping of rock and disappeared forever below the lake surface.

Not to be outdone, the *Nessen*, too, was caught on film after its demise came on that wretched night of the twenty-second. The striking photo shows the smokestack unseated and listing, and it would topple free from the ship. Her stern drooped as her hull fractured, and whitecap waves are pounding her. At the time Benson's ship made its unintended rendezvous with the lakebed of Pigeon Bay of Lake Erie, close to shore at Leamington, Ontario, the crew had made its way forward as the *Nessen* was then powerless. The crew comprised mostly of men from Detroit and Marine City, Michigan, and the ship's cook, Alice Humphrey, the only woman. The *Nessen* grounded about four hundred yards from shore.

Diminutive James Grubb of the Point Pelee Lifesaving Station was a featherweight at a 120 pounds. His efforts in rescuing the thirteen people aboard the *Nessen* made him a heavyweight in heroics. His station's lifeboat was loaded on a flatbed truck and driven to Leamington on Wednesday the twenty-third, arriving late that morning. Grubb's crew of two was augmented by the enlistment of six volunteers. The first effort to reach the *Nessen* was unsuccessful when one of the lifeboat's oarsmen lost his oar. Undaunted, Grubb and volunteers shoved off again. By noon, they reached the wrecked ship. Upon their arrival at the side of the *Nessen*, in the chill of the pilothouse, Alice Humphrey started to sing the song, "It Ain't Gonna Rain No More."

In the time-honored tradition, Benson was the last to leave the ship. The crowd that had assembled on the beach at Leamington roared their approval at Grubb and the volunteers' yeomanly work. The shipwrecked victims—the *Detroit News* reported it was Humphrey's second shipwreck in fifteen years—were served a meal and lodging at Leamington's Seacliffe Inn.

The scrap metal cargo the *Nessen* hauled was removed over time. The ship's saga had largely faded from memory by the spring of 1984. The Seacliffe Inn was still in business, as it is today. The spring of 1984 saw the dredging work commence on a new public marina at Leamington, and a hazard encountered were the *Nessen*'s remains. As sands that had long covered her remains were dredged and drag lines scraped across her disturbed grave, remnants of the ship were scooped up with the sand from the lake bottom and deposited on shore. A large portion of her prow and keel was salvaged, dropped off like a FedEx parcel on the site of a future parking lot.

A curious local youth, Chris Tassey, was sifting through the sand pile when he articulated the edge of a bell, a find he was uncertain of until he found the clapper. Someone from the construction crew ran him off, but when he related this story to his mom, she contacted Leamington mayor, John Penner. Penner intervened, and the bell was secured and saved. He praised Tassey, in the presence of the reporter from the *Leamington Post* on April 11, 1984, "It's a good thing you're curious, or the bell would have been buried under that parking lot with another pass of the bulldozer." The inscription on the bell, seventy-pounds of brass of finial flourish ordered by Root in 1880, reads: "Buckeye Foundry, Cincinnati C. W. Coffin."

Another local resident was carefully observing the operation at the marina site as remnants of the *Nessen* were unceremoniously dumped ashore. Robert McCracken, a farmer from Staples, Ontario, just north of Leamington, was a man passionate about local history. He was fascinated by the *Nessen* story, so as the large portion of her bow and keel lie on the beach, exposed to sun and the air for the first time in fifty-five years, he made the move of a committed lover of a historic relic: he had it moved to his farm property for safekeeping until a permanent solution to preserve the wreckage could be devised.

The bow and keel section of the ship was roughly twenty-one feet long and weighed several tons. It was placed aboard a flatbed trailer and was motored off to McCracken's farm. Timbers of framework and ribs were still quite solid, and some of the iron spikes used in her original construction had worked free from the breaks in the hull, like unruly needles from an oaken pin cushion. Not surprising, in view of the massive section of the *Nessen*'s remains, preservation would be a challenging proposition. How to, where to, and how much money to be invested into? As these questions awaited answer, the defiant prow of the archaic steamship sat behind the barn on McCracken's farm. It sat there for a long time. His grandchildren played in the wreckage—a retrieved shipwreck subbing as a jungle gym on fertile Canadian farmland. Years passed. Then decades. A mulberry tree took root and began growing through the *Nessen*'s shattered keel.

In 2011, McCracken decided it was time for the remains of the *Nessen* to find another home. Any hope for a permanent display place had disappeared, like so many hopeful years from the calendar. It was carted off to an unknown destination of equally unknown outcome. McCracken died in March of 2022. Just before he passed away, I spoke to him by phone. As we ended our conversation, he told me if there was anything left of the ship, he would gladly give it to me. I responded that I would gladly receive it.

The recovered bell was on display at the Leamington Public Library for several years, into the 1990s. Despite numerous emails to prospective leads in the whereabouts of the bell today, I was unable to ascertain the status of where it is housed and its ownership. The trail of the bell has gone cold, evaporated like so much Lake Erie water that covered it for years in Pigeon Bay.

The Advent of Tankers
on the Great Lakes

arnia, Ontario, is a likely location to begin excavations into the buried history of tankers on the Great Lakes. Conversely, the period, the autumn of 1862, and the ship, the barque *Thomas F. Park*, hardly so. In the first week of November, overhauled, fitted with a fresh set of canvas, the *Park*, under the command of Captain William B. Macleod, started down the St. Lawrence River with 1,700 barrels of oil, shipped at Sarnia. Five hundred barrels were consigned at Montreal, and the remaining cargo was bound for Falmouth, England. The *Park* had crossed the Atlantic before, on at least two occasions, but her cargo on those occasions, nearly as can be determined, wasn't oil. Indeed, this venture may not have been unquestionably the first lake boat to cross the Atlantic with barrels of refined crude oil pumped from the interior of North America, but it was surely among the earliest.

The voyage of the *Park*, serving as a precursor of tankers on the Great Lakes, is bound not only to the white oak barrels refined crude was shipped in. As methods and vessels evolved in transporting oil, crossing the Atlantic is integral as in telling this story as crossing Lake Erie would be. The developments from barrels to barges and finally to steamships transpired on both fresh and salt water.

Not surprising, the central powerful figures dominating nearly the entire stage of development and deployment as well as the oil itself was John D. Rockefeller Sr. and the Standard Oil Company monolith he built. Wedding the story of tankers and Rockefeller may elicit little in appealing imagery or nostalgic waxing. There is little warmth for either in the annals of history. For tankers specifically, and particularly those trading in the crude trade on the oceans, a legacy of appalling accidents and shipping disasters has tarred them with contempt. Globally, tanker catastrophes have caused unparalleled damage to beaches and wildlife when ships were doomed. Vessel names live in infamy with many to this day: *Torrey Canyon*, *Amoco Cadiz*, *Exxon Valdez*. When their hulls proved frangible and cracked like rusk, releasing tens of thousands of barrels of crude oil off the coasts of England, France, and Alaska, even after decades these black nightmares can still haunt sleep. On February 4, 1970, in Chedabucto Bay, on the east coast of Nova Scotia, the tanker *Arrow* ran aground on Cerberus Rock. The ship gutted itself, fouling over 150 miles of beach with bunker C oil, creating the worst oil spill in this part of the world. The *Arrow* had made trips into the Great Lakes in earlier years.

Whereas ocean-going crude oil tankers are disparate from Great Lakes tankers that carried refined crude oil blends, there, too, is a crossover. The genes running through both carry Rockefeller's DNA.

In Ron Chernow's splendid biography of Rockefeller, *Titan: The Life of John D. Rockefeller, Sr.*, he points out that in 1865, at the age of twenty-five, Rockefeller had control of Cleveland's largest refinery. He wrote, "From his new command post (2nd floor of a brick building on Superior Street, several blocks from the Cuyahoga) he could stare out the windows and follow the progress of barges drifting by laden with oil barrels from his refinery." The contents of those barrels were primarily refined crude, but they also contained kerosene and naphtha.

When the Cleveland-built schooner *Narragansett* sailed from the same place with an oil barrel load for Europe in 1867, it roamed the Atlantic and Caribbean, as well as the Gulf of Mexico for five years before returning to the lakes in August of 1872. In the autumn of 1868, the transatlantic trade in barreled oil from Cleveland spiked. On October 4, the barque *Wiralite* sailed for Liverpool with barrels of refined oil. A few days later, another barque, the *Etowah*, laden with 2,000 barrels of oil, stores, and boat oars, departed the city for the same destination. For the *Etowah*, like the *Park* before her, a transatlantic voyage was nothing new. The *Etowah*, formerly known as the *Howell Hoppock*, was roughed up during a stretch of bad weather on the Atlantic en route to Liverpool in the summer of 1863. On that trip, her cargo consisted of copper and barrel staves, not barreled oil, but her seaworthiness accorded her this new opportunity.

That same October would mark the occasion of an early catastrophe on the lakes in this inchoate stage of transporting barreled oil. On the twenty-fifth, having barely cleared Cleveland heavily laden with oil barrels, and bound for Europe, the *L. H. Cotton* caught fire. There were no injuries, but the *Cotton* was consumed by the fire, as was her cargo. The event raised suspicion. The *Cotton*, a 395-ton product of Cleveland's famed Quayle & Martin shipbuilding yard, was heavily insured by multiple carriers' policies written at Cincinnati the day before she sailed. The coincidence of the timing raised red flags, and litigation soon followed. A little over two years later, in December of 1870, a U.S. Circuit Court ruled in favor of a plaintiff in the flap, George W. Bissell, and claims were finally paid.

The Standard Oil Company was founded on January 10, 1870. The following year, Rockefeller's brother, Frank, controlled the steamer *Iron City*, which was moving oil barrels between Cleveland and Buffalo. The *Iron City* was yet another Quayle & Martin ship. Built in 1856, its dimensions were 185 feet in length, a beam of twenty-nine, and drew twelve feet of water. It featured longitudinal arches for hull strength, measured 611 tons, and was powered by two high pressure engines, turning twin ten-foot propellers. The *Iron City* may well have been the first vessel to carry the patent blue Standard Oil barrels following the company's formation. More important is what transpired the following year.

Between February 18 and March 25 of 1872, Rockefeller swallowed up his competitors in the refinery business in Cleveland in what became known as the "Cleveland Massacre." He now exerted solitary control over the city's massive refinery complex along the Cuyahoga River. From that point on, any oil product exported from Cleveland bore his ownership signature.

The Standard Oil product line was rapidly expanding by 1874. Technological advances and research and development branches were producing and marketing paraffin wax (for chewing gum, as well as other uses), lubricants, machine oils, tar oil for roadways, dyes, candles, and paints. It also marked the period when Rockefeller hired a crucial player and formidable figure in not only this story but also the entirety of the Standard Oil Company's history: Daniel O'Day. O'Day would lead the pipeline construction phase of the business, ultimately earning him the title of czar, in both friendly and hostile camps. Chernow called O'Day "a profane, two-fisted Irishman who tempered ruthless tactics with wit and charm."

The period of oil shipments in barrels was hardly without mishaps beyond the *Cotton* debacle. Ironically, the *Iron City* would be an early casualty. On September

25, 1872, then reduced to a barge, the vessel had been chartered to run oil barrels on the run she was familiar with, the Cleveland to Buffalo route. The *Iron City*'s captain was Richard Manning and was under tow of the tug *M. I. Mills* when things went awry. Winds steadily grew and reached gale strength, and with it, heavier seas. Off Point Abino, Ontario, the towline parted. *Iron City* was driven ashore, and while Manning and his crew of four survived, their barge was a total loss. There is nothing in the record to tell us how the oil barrels fared.

Identifying vessels in the transportation of barreled oil or kerosene was often revealed only through mishaps or accidents that resulted in leakage. Occasional cargoes link at least two of the Union Steamboat Line's iron-hulled propellers in moving oil barrels. The *Scotia* arrived at Milwaukee with a load on June 16, 1875. A sister ship, the *Java*, sailing under the Commercial Line banner, would have her own experience in the oil barrel trade two years later.

Abreast Point Pelee on angry Lake Erie, October 7, 1877, the *Java* was being pummeled by thundering seas. In water ballast, thus relatively light, the boat was carrying a cargo of stoves and flagstones, topped with a deck load of oil barrels. The *Java* would brook the lathering it endured, but forced into the trough of the seas, flagstones shattered and several stoves were demolished. Twenty barrels of oil were ruptured, cascading the amber liquid across her deck and over her sides. In reporting the frightening incident, the *Detroit Free Press* said, "The oil, which, by the way, was not stamped with any register to the fire test, as required by law, was consigned at Bay City." Pointing out the unmarked oil barrels in the *Java* incident sets the table for the perfect segue. A later oil barrel disaster gives strong indication that the horrors of the episode hastened the movement to change the transportation of oil byproducts to vessels designed specifically for the purpose of a safer liquid bulk cargo containment and shipment. But not before another mishap with the *Java* and her cargo of barreled petroleum products.

On August 18, 1878 off Little Point Sable on Lake Michigan, ten months after her shake-up on Lake Erie, disaster struck the ship. It is believed that the starboard propeller shaft of the twin-screw *Java* broke in half. The propeller dragged the shaft with it to the lake bottom. The opening in the shaft sleeve allowed inflowing water and doomed the ship, sinking the *Java* in over two hundred feet of water. There were no casualties in the incident, but it likely resulted in the first case of oil byproduct pollution on Lake Michigan.

Barrels of kerosene that comprised much of the boat's cargo ruptured, spreading a sheen over the lake. According to Captain Henry Reid of the schooner *Westcott*,

FIGURE 13. *Tioga* following deadly explosion in Chicago on July 11, 1890. From the Fr. Edward J. Dowling, S.J. Marine Historical Collection, University of Detroit Mercy.

cruising the scene of the *Java*'s demise, the kerosene was spread over a three-mile distance. By the end of August, one hundred intact barrels had been recovered.

On the sultry evening of July 11, 1890, the Union Steamboat Line's steel-hulled propeller *Tioga* reached her company dock on the Chicago River near the Randolph Street Bridge. In her aft hold, among other cargo to be unloaded, were one hundred barrels of oil, according to her captain, Austin Phelps. Around 7:30, stevedores and unloading personnel entered the close, dank petroleum-scented confines of the hold, and when a kerosene lamp was introduced to provide light, the aft end of the *Tioga* exploded like ordnance.

As the ship burned, thousands of Chicagoans crowded along the Randolph Street Bridge and vicinity, gazing in amazement. At least fourteen would die in the ghastly inferno, including eight African American Chicago-based stevedores.

Questioned by both the *Chicago Daily Inter-Ocean* and reported in the *Detroit Free Press* the day after the disaster on how the explosion could have happened, Phelps responded, "I have no idea what caused the oil to ignite. It may have been from one of the lamps, or spontaneous combustion." Unsatisfied with this answer, questions persisted about the probable cause. Phelps's rejoinder was, "No one can tell. We had no gasoline or naphtha aboard. We did have one hundred barrels of crude petroleum, but that would not have exploded."

The bill of goods Phelps was sold originated with the shippers of the "oil," the Genesee Oil Company of Buffalo, New York. He was honest in his statements; to his knowledge the product he was shipping in the barrels was oil. Alas, it was not oil, but rather it was naphtha, and the deadly conflagration would have been avoided with proper labeling.

The year after the *Tioga* explosion, a seminal work project was underway at the American Steel Barge Company yard at Superior, Wisconsin. Important as it was, ambiguity surrounded the genesis of the mission. If by fiat or closed board meeting decision, whether Rockefeller himself was entirely responsible or persuaded, he certainly enabled the event to be orchestrated. On July 29, 1891, at the shipyard famous for turning out Alexander McDougall's iconic whalebacks, the Standard Oil Company launched its first oil barge on the Great Lakes. Not only was it the first on the Great Lakes, but it may have been the first built in North America. It was unquestionably one of them. This natal, radical development was not only surprisingly low-key and off the radar but also utterly no imagination went into naming the breakthrough craft. It was given a generic, plain-vanilla name: *S. O. Co. No. 55.*

The *55* was 155 feet in length, 30 feet in beam, and drew 10 feet of water. Separated into three tanks that stretched 96 feet of her hull, *55* could carry roughly 400,000 gallons of oil. This triumphant accomplishment resulted in a quick parade down the lakes, and then an exit from them. Towed by another recent launch from the McDougall yard, the whaleback steamer *E. B. Bartlett*, and both on their maiden voyages, the *55* was dropped off at Port Colborne, Ontario. After being towed through the Welland Canal and the St. Lawrence River, the barge was put into service for Standard Oil Company on the Atlantic Ocean trade. This stanza of correlation of advancements in tanker evolution on the Great Lakes and the Atlantic operations was merely another link in the chain.

Even with the *55*'s success on the Atlantic coastal trade, it was years before a progeny of oil barges would be constructed. The year 1895 proved to be one of triumphant breakthroughs for the Standard Oil Company. Not only would the next generation of oil barges be born, it would also mark the occasion of the first shipment of refined crude oil products from their fledgling Whiting, Indiana, refinery.

The discovery of the oil fields of northwest Ohio and northern Indiana, near Lima, Ohio, in May of 1885 (henceforth the Lima–Indiana field), foretold the future of tankers that would one day ply the Great Lakes. The oil extracted from the Lima–Indiana field was problematic for Standard Oil. Heavily sulfurous and repulsively smelly, it was a far cry from eastern crude oil they were accustomed to refining. The challenge of solving this dilemma fell to another Rockefeller hire—a German-born chemist named Herman Frasch. Referred to as a "mad scientist" or the "Flying Dutchman," Frasch's brilliance in devising a method to remove the sulfur would be dubbed the "Herman Vapor Process" in the nomenclature of Standard Oil men.

Solving the sour crude issue, O'Day and his voracious pipeline tonging crew would connect the Lima–Indiana fields to the Lake Michigan port city of Whiting, Indiana. The fruits of their labor, sweetened crude piped to the shores of the most populated Great Lake, would be further refined there for years, even generations, to come.

Early in 1895, the American Steel Barge Company's Superior yard again answered the call for a tank oil barge. On May 11, at five o'clock sharp, Standard Oil's "schooner" *S. O. No. 75* was launched. Mandated by insurance agencies to carry sails, the steel-hulled *75* was equipped with nine thousand feet of canvas to spread. The *75* was larger than her predecessor *55* by roughly forty-five feet—170 feet in overall length. Her beam of thirty-one feet was similar to the *55*, and the ten-foot draft was also. Her capacity, reported in the *Detroit Free Press*, was listed as like that of the *55*, but surely was more. The *75* was divided into eight compartments.

The deployment of *75* continued the advancement in the oil tank barge experiment. Monitoring the movements of the latest barge was a peak interest to Standard Oil and shipping concerns throughout the lakes. Whatever trials and tribulations they would sail through in this nascent stage, their existence from this point on was connected to the pipeline at Whiting, which was nearing completion.

The *75* was towed to South Chicago by the whaleback steamer *A. D. Thomson*. There, for a fortnight, it patiently waited on the completion of the pipeline at Whiting. From the shore at Whiting, a pier carrying the necessary pipes connecting the refinery pumps to anchored vessels was several hundred feet short of its 1,500 feet destination length. Shortage of materials delayed the project's finish. We can imagine the creatively acidic strings of profanity O'Day mouthed as he impatiently waited on construction materials.

At last, on July 20, 1895, the *75* was filled with 6,000 barrels of oil, destined for a Duluth, Minnesota, delivery. It consummated the first shipment from the Standard Oil refinery at Whiting. The measurement in barrels, not gallons, was the first notation of this capacity I found in the study of tankers. O'Day may have calmed, but even this advancement in the shipment of petroleum products left much to be desired.

As the *75* was under tow and making its way for Duluth, a second Standard Oil barge was launched at the American Steel Barge complex at Superior. On June 4, *S. O. No. 76* was ready for service. When departing Superior, *76* provided observers a fantastic, probably one-off opportunity to behold: *76* raised canvas to the wind and, sans any assistance not provided by the elements, sailed to the Soo.

Despite the significant roles oil barges *75* and *76* played in the development of tankers on the lakes, there are no known photographs of either. Not even drawings. Thankfully, marine news correspondents from the *Detroit Free Press* were carefully monitoring these peculiar new interlopers. According to a detailed report in the June 5 edition,

> The barges carry electric lights that are vapor proof, so that there is no danger of an explosion or fire from them even when naphtha is being carried. Two large pumps in the forward part of the boat are used to discharge the cargo, and when these are run at full capacity the cargo of 10,000 barrels can be discharged in six hours. A double bulkhead between the boiler room and the oil tanks is kept full of water all the time as a protection against fire. The two barges, or, more properly, schooners, are being towed by tugs belonging to the Saginaw Bay Towing Association.

This insight adds plumage in dressing out the early tank barge operations. From the point of entry into service and when tugboats were not available, *75* and *76* would also hitchhike tows behind ore boats, catching a lift when it presented itself. Unfortunately, it could also mean long delays in the process.

There were many more Standard Oil barges to follow. Some of the tugs to tow the barges have been identified, including the *Lutz*, *Chauncey A. Morgan*, and the Canadian workhorse, *Reginald*. Years would pass before an idea, proposed in the *Detroit Free Press*'s September 10, 1895, edition, would come to fruition on the Great Lakes: "Marine men think the best scheme for the company is to build a large tank steamer which will be able to tow the barges and also carry a good load of oil in bulk."

The Tyne Iron Shipbuilding Company's Willington Quay yard, on River Tyne, England, wasn't far from the North Sea. On January 22, 1898, a composite steel and iron-hulled creation took to the waters of River Tyne. It wasn't particularly large, a mere two hundred feet in length, thirty-two feet in beam, and drawing a bit over fifteen feet of water. It was powered by a triple expansion steam engine (17, 26, and 45" × 30") that turned a single propeller. The ship, a tanker, was named *Minoco*. A few years later it would usher in a new era on the lakes.

By the end of the nineteenth century, two Canadian entities marketed by the Standard Oil Company—Imperial Oil Company Ltd. and Anglo-American Oil Company Ltd.—were purchased outright, becoming the first fully integrated affiliate outside of the borders of the United States to be controlled by Standard Oil. In 1901, Anglo-American's London-based operation purchased the *Minoco* and renamed the ship *Imperial.* The following year the tanker would cross the Atlantic and begin operating on the Great Lakes.

The *Imperial*'s lines would serve as a template for marine architecture for tankers for years to come. A bluff bow, clean lines in the sheer strake of the bow, was followed by forward tanks. A midship cabin block and navigation bridge were followed by another tank deck, leading to the aft cabins above the engine room, finished off with a shapely contoured counter stern.

On Tuesday night, May 6, 1902, with Standard Oil barge *86* in tow from the Atlantic Ocean, the *Imperial* docked at Cleveland for the first time. It isn't clear if Rockefeller paid a courtesy or business call in visiting the first self-propelled tanker to operate on the Great Lakes. Nor is there clear evidence any Standard Oil Company representative called on the ship as it rode the Cuyahoga River. Hastily engaged in the oil trade on the lakes, the *Imperial* was an instant success. This same year would see another milestone reached in tanker development. The scene of this breakthrough would come a bit farther west along the lakeshore of Ohio, at Toledo, and the yard of the Toledo Shipbuilding Company.

The year before, near Beaumont, Texas, a Vesuvian eruption of viscus, tar-black crude rose from the bowels of the earth. This geyser of ebony gold, "Texas Tea," marked a new era of oil fields and impending wealth in the United States, and the name associated with the site would be iconic and unique so as not to be confused with anything else: Spindletop.

The infant Texas Oil Company was in dire need of a tank ship to transport just a scintilla of the output of Spindletop once the gusher's flow was piped to a Gulf of Mexico port. They contracted with the Toledo Shipbuilding Company for such a ship, aware of the size limitations warranted by the Welland Canal locks, through which the ship must pass, as did the *Imperial*. The canal locks could accommodate a vessel of maximum length of 260 feet, so the plans called for the tank steamer to measure 256 feet in overall length. The ship wouldn't be named for anything related to Texas or to oil: it was christened *Toledo*. Like Standard Oil barges 75 and 76, there are no known photographs of the ship, despite the significant groundbreaking construction of these trail-blazing vessels.

The naval architectural blueprints of the *Toledo* do exist, and are housed at Bowling Green, Ohio, in the Historical Collections of the Great Lakes at Bowling Green State University. They are magnificent. The *Toledo* was powered by a triple expansion engine (21, 34, and 57" × 40") fed by two Scotch boilers fourteen feet in diameter and twelve feet long, generating a 170 pounds of steam. Her hull was divided into twelve compartments, six on each side of the cabin block, and navigation bridge, giving the ship a capacity of over one million gallons. The design would allow the *Toledo* to carry multiple refined products. To be expected of blueprints and their concise nature, it can be seen that the *Toledo*'s capacious icebox was twice the size of the quarters shared by three of the ship's oilers.

Under the command of Captain M. W. Humphrey, the *Toledo* passed downbound on the Welland Canal on November 12, 1902, bound for Philadelphia. The city would become her homeport, even with her runs from Texas laden with the gift of Spindletop to eastern port cities. Here again we see the dovetailing of oil trade and craft on the Atlantic and the lakes. As the British-built *Imperial* worked as the first self-propelled tanker to operate on the lakes, the first American-produced tanker on the lakes exited for the Atlantic and the Gulf of Mexico.

The *Imperial* worked the lakes for several years. Often towing Standard Oil barges, sometimes sailing solo, Cleveland and Sarnia would punctuate her agendas. And she was fast. According to the *Detroit Free Press*, she could reach the speed of eighteen miles an hour. This put her in the class of most crack passenger liners of the era, but slower than the speedsters *City of Erie* and *Tashmoo*, the fastest vessels on the lakes. Her frequent transits of the Welland Canal would become a thing of

FIGURE 14. *Imperial* in the Welland Canal. From the Fr. Edward J. Dowling, S.J. Marine Historical Collection, University of Detroit Mercy.

legend in the 1903 shipping season. When the season finally ended, the sedulous *Imperial* had logged a gaudy, perhaps unprecedented forty-two transits in the canal.

While the *Imperial* and tug and barge combos toiled in the movements of oil and assorted refined crude products in the opening decade of the twentieth century, the development and popularity of the automobile and motor trucks would redefine the oil industry. In 1910, for the first time, gasoline became the chief byproduct of demand since the inception of crude oil refining. The gasoline-powered internal combustion engine was changing the world, and gasoline, once a pesky, dangerous, ubiquitous nuisance, became an unimaginable windfall of wealth. Rockefeller himself would speak to the abundance of the unwanted gasoline as it was unabashedly allowed to flow directly into the Cuyahoga River at his monolithic refinery complex. "We used to burn it for fuel in distilling the oil, and thousands, hundreds of thousands of barrels of it floated down the creeks and rivers, and the ground was saturated with it in the constant effort to get rid of it," he claimed.

The demand for gasoline resulted in the need for expansion in the number of vessels to carry it, both barges and steamships. Standard Oil would lead the charge, and 1911 proved to be a prolific year in construction of both along the lakes, for needs regionally and beyond. The linkage of lake-built craft to Atlantic Ocean service remained intact. It prompted a marine news columnist from the *Detroit Free Press* to write on August 2 of that year, "Probably never before in the history of lake shipbuilding have so many boats for salt water been under construction at lake yards at the same time." What had occurred in May established another watershed in the annals of tankers and the Great Lakes.

On the twenty-first of the month, the steamer *Perfection* was launched from Cleveland. In perfect symmetry with Standard Oil and Rockefeller's domain—for years the Cleveland refinery was Standard's most prolific in production—the birthplace of the first United States–built tanker on the Great Lakes to serve on the Great Lakes, was felicitous. The dimensions of the *Perfection*, 260 feet overall length, 43 feet in beam, and a draft of 20, like predecessors, was built with transits of the Welland Canal in mind. The tanker was powered by a triple expansion engine (19, 31, and 54″ × 42″) with twin Scotch boilers, 14½ feet in diameter and 11½ feet long, capable of 200 pounds of steam. Unlike its predecessors, the *Perfection* was built in the style of conventional lake boats, with forward wheelhouse, deck length and engine and aft cabins on the stern. In essence, it was a prototype of lakes-built tankers to come. Immediately after the *Perfection* launch, construction on her duplicate, the *Eocene*, commenced.

With a plume of smoke like black cotton candy billowing from her funnel, the *Perfection* was observed as she passed Detroit, upbound on her first trip. The tanker was bound for Whiting where her first cargo, kerosene, was guzzled aboard. The cargo was slated for delivery at Duluth, but before the ship would arrive, the ceremonious occasion was clipped; there was a fly in the ointment. For reasons unclear, the tanker called on Mackinaw City, Michigan, where samples of her cargo were taken. Reports claimed it was flawed, inappropriately off-color and inferior, and the *Perfection* was sent back to Whiting with it. This rain on the *Perfection*'s parade was only a temporary shower. For the remainder of the shipping season, the tanker would be paired with various Standard Oil barges. Often, they would carry different refined product cargoes, the ship with kerosene and a barge topped off with gasoline. The *Perfection* would unload first, often steaming away with an

Perfection Oil Steamer at Aransas Pass, Texas.

FIGURE 15. *Perfection* had a crucial but short career on the Lakes. Courtesy of the Alpena County George N. Fletcher Library, Alpena, Michigan.

empty barge, rather than waiting for her loaded consort to be unloaded, thus not idly wasting hours in port.

The *Eocene* was launched on September 16, but the newsworthiness was overshadowed by the announcement of the largest tanker ever to be built on the Great Lakes. Slated for construction at the Lorain, Ohio, yard of the American Shipbuilding Company over the ensuing winter, anticipation was great for the scheduled spring launching. May of 1912 would see an unparalleled success to the Standard Oil Company holdings, but not before enduring a horrific tragedy.

On May 1, at the refinery complex at the foot of Jefferson Street, on the Cuyahoga, Standard Oil barge *S. O. No. 88* was slurping aboard a load of gasoline. Alongside was another company barge, undergoing caulking procedures being carried out by employees of the Great Lakes Towing Company. Their company tugs, *Wisconsin* and *Pennsylvania*, were also pulled up to the site. Bisecting the city, the Cuyahoga River had long been debased by heavy industry, reducing it to a torpid, toxic stream. In the bouillabaisse of pollutants, the Standard Oil refinery added to the river's woes with inflammableness. On that day, for the fourth time in history, the combustible, oily sheen smothering the river caught fire. In fleeting seconds, the blaze reached the *88*, setting off an explosion and horrific inferno. Five men caulking the adjacent barge, Louis Gale and his son, Frank, Felix Boucher, Nelson Levere, and Albert Marquise, were incinerated. In the aftermath of the blaze, the charred tugs and barges were a grim reminder of the disaster, floating in mute testimony of the Cuyahoga's sad, potentially deadly state.

The saturnine mourning period for the workers in the marine transportation division of Standard Oil would brighten somewhat over the next few weeks. A joyous breakthrough finally came on May 20, not at Cleveland, but Lorain. James Kilpatrick, marine manager for the Standard Oil fleet of Great Lakes operations, sponsored the launching of the enormous tanker *Renown*. The ship was a giant tanker for her time, 390 feet in length, 52 feet in beam, and a thirsty draft of 25 feet. The largesse of the *Renown*'s impressive numbers meant specifically one thing: she was too large to negotiate the Welland Canal—the *Renown* was built to *stay* on the lakes. Her capacity in gallons was also impressive: 2,659,600. Emulating the largest bulk carrier lake boats of the era, her forward wheelhouse and accommodations were trailed by a long, uninterrupted cargo deck, concluding at her aft end cabins and smokestack over her engine room, enhanced by her sculpted, appealing counter stern.

On July 19, under the watchful eye and direction of Captain William J. Lynn, 1,750,000 gallons of oil in her gut and barge *86* in tow—the same *86* the *Imperial* was towing when she made her way into the Great Lakes for the first time ten years earlier—*Renown* sailed from Cleveland on her maiden voyage. It is worth noting, despite the objective of this chapter being the advent of tankers on the lakes, the *Renown*, twice renamed and finishing off her career as the *Mercury* for the Cleveland Tankers fleet, sailed for over sixty years before being broken up.

Arbitrarily ending this chapter on the genesis of tankers plying the waters of the Great Lakes, the Canadian framework in this chapter will serve as bookends. Whereas the story begins there, so too shall it end. Not at Sarnia, however, rather Collingwood, Ontario. On December 15, 1915, at Collingwood, Margaret Hanna, daughter of Ontario Provincial Secretary William J. Hanna, christened the tanker *Royalite*. The ship's splash into the waters of Georgian Bay would add another first to this tale while also concluding it: the *Royalite* was the first Canadian-built tanker to sail the Great Lakes.

Bibliography

THE *LADY ELGIN*, 1859

"Arriving from Liverpool." *Detroit Free Press*, October 13, 1859.

"A Steamer Disabled." *Detroit Free Press*, November 22, 1859.

Boyer, Dwight. *True Tales of the Great Lakes*. New York: Dodd, Mead & Company, New York, 1971.

"Clearing For Foreign Ports." *Chicago Tribune*, May 16, 1859.

"Collision with an Iceberg." *Detroit Free Press*, September 23, 1859.

"For Europe." *Detroit Free Press*, May 14, 1859.

"From Lake Superior." *Chicago Tribune*, May 18, 1859.

"From Lake Superior." *Chicago Tribune*, August 2, 1859.

"From Lake Superior." *Chicago Tribune*, October 18, 1859.

"The Lady Elgin." *Chicago Tribune*, April 21, 1859.

"The Lady Elgin." *Chicago Tribune*, December 1, 1859.

"Marine Disaster at the Straits." *Chicago Tribune*, April 20, 1859.

"Marine Intelligence." *Chicago Tribune*, April 12, 1859.

"Marine Intelligence." *Chicago Tribune*, May 2, 1859.

"Marine Intelligence." *Chicago Tribune*, June 8, 1859.

"Marine Intelligence." *Chicago Tribune*, June 10, 1859.

"Marine Intelligence." *Chicago Tribune*, June 13, 1859.

"Marine Intelligence." *Chicago Tribune*, July 22, 1859.

"Marine Intelligence." *Chicago Tribune*, October 4, 1859.

"Marine Intelligence." *Chicago Tribune*, November 7, 1859.

"Port of Chicago." *Chicago Tribune*, July 4, 1859.

"Port of Chicago." *Chicago Tribune*, August 3, 1859.

"Port of Chicago." *Chicago Tribune*, August 15, 1859.

"Port of Chicago." *Chicago Tribune*, August 26, 1859.

"Port of Chicago." *Chicago Tribune*, November 12, 1859.

"Steamer Lady Elgin." *Chicago Tribune*, October 22, 1859.

"Steamer Lady Elgin." *Chicago Tribune*, November 25, 1859.

"Trip of the Lady Elgin." *Chicago Tribune*, May 20, 1859.

"Untitled." *Chicago Tribune*, May 21, 1859.

DETROIT TO CONSTANTINOPLE

"A Coaster from the Lakes." *Detroit Free Press*, April 20, 1860.

"A Lake Vessel for Boston." *Chicago Tribune*, August 30, 1859.

"Another Vessel for England." *Chicago Tribune*, May 29, 1858.

"Another Vessel for Europe." *Chicago Tribune*, June 16, 1859.

"Another Vessel for Spain." *Chicago Tribune*, May 10, 1859.

"Arrived at Richmond; Arrived at Constantinople." *Chicago Tribune*, November 16, 1859.

"Arrival from Liverpool." *Chicago Tribune*, July 1, 1857.

"Arriving from Liverpool." *Detroit Free Press*, October 13, 1859.

"Arrival of the R. H. Harmon." *Detroit Free Press*, September 23, 1859.

"The Bark C. J. Kershaw." *Detroit Free Press*, May 30, 1858.

"The Bark D. C. Pierce." *Detroit Free Press*, May 22, 1858.

"The Bark Kershaw." *Detroit Free Press*, June 6, 1858.

"The Brig Black Hawk." *Chicago Tribune*, June 28, 1859.

"Chicago and Liverpool." *Detroit Free Press*, July 22, 1856.

"The Cleveland Herald Says." *Chicago Tribune*, August 5, 1859.

Defebaugh, James Elliott. *History of the Lumber Industry of America*. Vol. 2. Chicago: American
    Lumberman, 1907.

"Direct Trade with Liverpool." *Detroit Free Press*, May 23, 1858.

"First Arrival of the Foreign Fleet." *Chicago Tribune*, September 8, 1859.

"First Vessel for Liverpool This Season." *Detroit Free Press*, May 6, 1858.

"For Europe." *Chicago Tribune*, April 30, 1859.

"For Europe." *Chicago Tribune*, May 14, 1859.

"For Europe." *Chicago Tribune*, June 13, 1859.

"For Europe." *Detroit Free Press*, April 11, 1860.

"For Ireland Direct." *Chicago Tribune*, June 9, 1859.

"For Liverpool." *Detroit Free Press*, August 1, 1857.

"For Liverpool." *Detroit Free Press*, August 19, 1857.

"For Liverpool." *Detroit Free Press*, May 9, 1858.

"For Liverpool." *Chicago Tribune*, May 15, 1858.

"For Liverpool." *Detroit Free Press*, May 14, 1859.

"For Ocean Trade; For Europe." *Chicago Tribune*, May 26, 1859.

"Four More Vessels for Europe." *Chicago Tribune*, April 14, 1859.

"From Liverpool Direct." *Detroit Free Press*, October 11, 1859.

"Getting Ready for Europe." *Detroit Free Press*, April 22, 1860.

"The G. D. Douseman." *Chicago Tribune*, July 26, 1859.

"Ho! For the Salt, Salt Sea." *Chicago Tribune*, August 20, 1859.

"Lake and Ocean Direct Trade." *Chicago Tribune*, July 15, 1859.

"Lake and Ocean Direct Trade." *Detroit Free Press*, April 28, 1860.

"Lake and Ocean Trade." *Chicago Tribune*, August 9, 1859.

"Lake Clippers." *Chicago Tribune*, November 10, 1859.

"Lake Fleet." *Chicago Tribune*, August 23, 1859.

"Lake Vessel Abandoned at Sea." *Detroit Free Press*, August 18, 1860.

"Lake Vessels for the Atlantic Ocean." *Detroit Free Press*, August 8, 1860.

"Loaded for Spain." *Chicago Tribune*, August 15, 1859.

"The Madera Pet." *Detroit Free Press*, August 13, 1857.

"Marine Intelligence." *Detroit Free Press*, June 13, 1858.

Marine Record, July 1, 1886.

Marine Record, July 8, 1886.

"More Foreign Vessels; Off for Europe." *Chicago Tribune*, May 9, 1959.

"Movements of the Lakes-Atlantic Fleet." *Chicago Tribune*, June 11, 1859.

"News of the Cleveland Fleet at Constantinople." *Chicago Tribune*, November 21, 1859.

"Our Vessels in Europe." *Detroit Free Press*, September 29, 1859.

"Quayle, Thomas." Encyclopedia of Cleveland, Case Western Reserve University, 1997–. https://
    case.edu/ech/articles/q/quayle-thomas.

"The Returning Fleet; A New Ocean Vessel." *Chicago Tribune*, August 22, 1859.

"Schooner R. H. Harmon." *Chicago Tribune*, September 1, 1859.

"Schooner St. Helena." *Chicago Tribune*, December 9, 1859.

"Started for Europe." *Detroit Free Press*, April 19, 1860.

"Trip of the Schooner Helena." *Chicago Tribune*, August 1, 1859.

U.S. Department of the Treasury, Bureau of Statistics. *List of Merchant Vessels of the United States*. U.S. Department of the Treasury: Washington, DC, 1869.

"Untitled." *Chicago Tribune*, April 22, 1856.

"Untitled." *Chicago Tribune*, August 1, 1856.

"Untitled." *Chicago Tribune*, August 8, 1856.

"Untitled." *Detroit Free Press*, August 16, 1857.

"Untitled." *Detroit Free Press*, August 21, 22, 23, 1857.

"Untitled." *Detroit Free Press*, August 26, 1857.

"Untitled." *Detroit Free Press*, September 22, 23, 1857.

"Untitled." *Detroit Free Press*, May 18, 1858.

"Untitled." *Detroit Free Press*, June 9, 1858.

"Untitled." *Chicago Tribune*, May 16, 1859.

"Untitled." *Detroit Free Press*, October 30, 1859.

"The Vessels for Liverpool from Detroit and Vicinity." *Chicago Tribune*, May 1, 1858.

"Vessels For Spain." *Chicago Tribune*, May 7, 1859.

DOPPELGANGERS TO THE BITTER END

"Amazing Novelty." *Detroit Free Press*, September 26, 1867.

"A Rough Passage." *Detroit Free Press*, September 25, 1872.

"Copper Recovered." *Detroit Free Press*, July 1, 1867.

"Copper Recovered." *Detroit Free Press*, August 1, 1867.

"Disaster." *Cleveland Plain Dealer*, September 17, 1873.

"Excursion on the Ironsides to Port Stanley and London." *Cleveland Plain Dealer*, August 8, 1867.

"From Milwaukee." *Detroit Free Press*, April 23, 1873.

"From Lake Superior." *Detroit Free Press*, August 16, 1864.

"From Lake Superior." *Detroit Free Press*, October 5, 1864.

"From Lake Superior." *Detroit Free Press*, May 22, 1866.

"From Lake Superior." *Detroit Free Press*, June 30, 1866.

"From Lake Superior." *Detroit Free Press*, July 28, 1866.

"Grand Lake Superior Excursion." *Cleveland Plain Dealer*, June 13, 1867.

"Ice At Milwaukee." *Detroit Free Press*, April 23, 1873.

"Immense Mackinac Trout." *Cleveland Plain Dealer*, September 24, 1866.

"The Ironsides." *Chicago Tribune*, September 21, 1873.

"The Lac La Belle Disaster." *Cleveland Plain Dealer*, November 26, 1866.

"The Lac La Belle." *Chicago Inter-Ocean*, October 16, 1872.

"The Lac La Belle." *Milwaukee Sentinel*, October 17, 1872.

"The Lac La Belle." *Chicago Inter-Ocean*, October 26, 1872.

"Loss of the Lac La Belle." *Milwaukee Sentinel*, October 16, 1872.

"Lake Superior News." *Detroit Free Press*, August 3, 1864.

"Launch of the New Steamer Ironsides." *Cleveland Plain Dealer*, July 25, 1864.

"Marine Disasters." *Chicago Tribune*, November 4, 1873.

"Marine Intelligence." *Chicago Inter-Ocean*, October 17, 1872.

"Milwaukee Bay Navigable by Foot." *Detroit Free Press*, April 25, 1873.

"More about the Sinking of the Lac La Belle." *Cleveland Plain Dealer*, November 28, 1866.

"The New Steamer Lac La Belle." *Cleveland Plain Dealer*, July 6, 1864.

"The New Steamer Lac La Belle—Engineer's Trial Trip." *Cleveland Plain Dealer*, July 8, 1864.

Project Shipshape. Ship Information and Data Record, *Ironsides* and *Lac La Belle*, Great Lakes Historical Collection, Milwaukee Public Library.

"Propeller Ironsides." *Cleveland Plain Dealer*, April 25, 1868.

"Propeller Ironsides." *Cleveland Plain Dealer*, June 17, 1868.

"Recovery of Copper." *Detroit Free Press*, August 1, 1867.

"Return of the Ironsides." *Cleveland Plain Dealer*, August 5, 1867.

"Sale of the Lac La Belle." *Cleveland Plain Dealer*, September 25, 1869.

"Singular Proceeding." *Cleveland Plain Dealer*, September 1, 1869.

"Sinking of the Lac La Belle." *Cleveland Plain Dealer*, November 25, 1866.

"The Situation at Milwaukee." *Detroit Free Press*, April 26, 1873.

"Steamship Milwaukee." *Detroit Free Press*, November 18, 1866.

"Untitled." *Cleveland Plain Dealer*, May 7, 1864.

"Untitled." *Detroit Free Press*, July 12, 13, 1864.

"Untitled." *Detroit Free Press*, July 12, 1866.

"Untitled." *Detroit Free Press*, September 3, 1866.

"Untitled." *Detroit Free Press*, November 23, 1866.

"Untitled." *Cleveland Plain Dealer*, August 1, 1869.

"Untitled." *Cleveland Plain Dealer*, October 2, 1872.

"Untitled." *Chicago Inter-Ocean*, November 7, 1872.

"Untitled." *Chicago Inter-Ocean*, November 14, 1872.

"Untitled." *Chicago Tribune*, September 16–18, 1873.

THE ICE-BUCKING STEAMSHIP *AURANIA*

"Algomah Did Great Work." *Detroit Free Press*, April 20, 1905.

"Andaste Damaged." *Detroit Free Press*, April 30, 1905.

"Aurania Breaks All Cargo Records." *Detroit Free Press*, September 14, 1895.

"Battle with Ice for Twenty Lives." *Cleveland Plain Dealer*, May 3, 1909.

"Big Aurora Burned." *Detroit Free Press*, December 13, 1898.

"Broke Her Own Record." *Detroit Free Press*, October 9, 1895.

"Chili Aground." *Detroit Free Press*, June 3, 1904.

"Cleveland Boat Goes Down in Ice." *Cleveland Plain Dealer*, April 30, 1909.

"Favorite Broke the Ice." *Detroit Free Press*, May 2, 1901.

"From Port Huron to Algonac." *Detroit Free Press*, April 29, 1901.

"Great Engineering Feat." *Detroit Free Press*, May 2, 1899.

"Ice Bucking Is Expensive." *Detroit Free Press*, April 21, 1905.

"In the Fog." *Cleveland Plain Dealer*, August 17, 1899.

Helgeson, Jeffrey. "American Labor and Working Class History, 1900–1945." Oxford Research Encyclopedia of American History, August 31, 2016. https://doi.org/10.1093/acrefore/9780199329175.013.330.

"Lame Ducks; That Ice Blockade." *Detroit Free Press*, December 12, 1898.

"Marine Notes." *Detroit Free Press*, September 1, 1895.

"Marine Notes." *Detroit Free Press*, September 3, 1895.

"Marine Notes." *Detroit Free Press*, October 8, 1895.

"Marine Notes." *Detroit Free Press*, November 27, 1895.

"Marine Notes." *Detroit Free Press*, April 9, 1899.

"Marine Notes." *Detroit Free Press*, April 19, 1899.

"Marine Notes." *Detroit Free Press*, May 7, 1899.

"Marine Notes." *Detroit Free Press*, May 4, 1901.

"Marine Notes." *Detroit Free Press*, May 9, 1901.

"Marine Notes." *Detroit Free Press*, May 18, 1904.

"Marine Notes." *Detroit Free Press*, June 2, 1904.

"Marine Notes." *Detroit Free Press*, June 12, 1904.

"Old Idea Revamped." *Detroit Free Press*, May 8, 1899.

"Preparing for the Season on the Lakes." *Detroit Free Press*, March 26, 1899.

"Same Ones at Amherstburg." *Detroit Free Press*, December 11, 1898.

"Schooner Aurania in Dock." *Detroit Free Press*, July 30, 1898.

"Steamer's Crew Saved from Ice." *Cleveland Plain Dealer*, May 1, 1909.

"The Straits Are Open." *Detroit Free Press*, April 19, 1905.

"Sunk Near the Flats." *Detroit Free Press*, July 25, 1898.

"Untitled." *Detroit Free Press*, December 17, 1898.

"Untitled." *Detroit Free Press*, April 30, 1901.

"Untitled." *Detroit Free Press*, May 1, 1901.

"Untitled." *Detroit Free Press*, May 4, 1901.

"Will Use an Ice Crusher; Aurania First; Ice Conditions." *Detroit Free Press*, April 18, 1905.

BONEYARD ON THE DETROIT RIVER

Adler, Richard. *Cholera in Detroit: A History*. Jefferson, NC: McFarland, 2013.

Advertisement. *Detroit Free Press*, June 10, 1884.

"The Artists Have Completed the Work on the Milton D Ward." *Detroit Free Press*, April 15, 1884.

"Bark Maria Martin." *Detroit Free Press*, November 16, 1870.

"Bark Maria Martin on Reef." *Chicago Tribune*, November 17, 1870.

"Collision." *Detroit Free Press*, June 23, 1866.

"Dorrington Routs Wrecker's Fleet." *Detroit Free Press*, June 17, 1910.

"Dorrington Will Continue Battle." *Detroit Free Press*, June 19, 1910.

The Federal Reporter: Vol. 121, *Cases Argued and Dismissed in the Circuit Court of Appeals and Circuit Courts of the United States*. St. Paul, MN: West Publishing Co., 1903.

"Fire on the Milton D Ward." *Detroit Free Press*, August 17, 1894.

Frederickson, Arthur C., and Lucy F. Frederickson. *Pictorial History of the C & O Train and Auto Ferries and Pere Marquette Line Steamers*. Rev. ed. Ludington, MI: Lakeside, 1965.

"Hackett to Move Schooner Martin." *Detroit Free Press*, June 15, 1910.

"In Dry Dock." *Detroit Free Press*, November 17, 1870.

"Lake Marine News." *Detroit Free Press*, May 21, 1908.

"Lake Marine News." *Detroit Free Press*, June 7, 1908.

Mansfield, John Brandt. *History of the Great Lakes*. 2 vols. Chicago: J. H. Beers & Co., 1899. https://catalog.hathitrust.org/Record/003931870.

"Marine News." *Detroit Free Press*, May 21, 1908.

"Marine Notes." *Detroit Free Press*, April 15, 1866.

"Marine Notes." *Detroit Free Press*, May 20, 1870.

"Marine Notes." *Detroit Free Press*, December 2, 1871.

"Marine Notes." *Detroit Free Press*, May 4, 1875.

"Marine Notes." *Detroit Free Press*, May 26, 1875.

"Marine Notes." *Detroit Free Press*, May 29, 1875.

"Marine Notes." *Detroit Free Press*, June 10, 1884.

"Marine Notes." *Detroit Free Press*, June 12, 1884.

"Marine Notes." *Detroit Free Press*, June 14, 1884.

"Marine Notes." *Detroit Free Press*, May 15, 1886.

"Marine Notes." *Detroit Free Press*, September 10, 11, 1886.

"Marine Notes." *Detroit Free Press*, September 24, 1886.

"Marine Notes." *Detroit Free Press*, April 21, 1899.

"Martin Is Taken to Amherstburg." *Detroit Free Press*, June 18, 1910.

"Milton D. Ward." *Detroit Free Press*, April 8, 1888.

"The New Steamer." *Detroit Free Press*, June 1, 1870.

"The Old Jay Cooke." *Detroit Free Press*, August 28, 1895.

"The River Route." *Detroit Free Press*, April 12, 1873.

"Schooner Wm. Jones." *Detroit Free Press*, November 18, 1866.

"Starvation on the Lakes." *Detroit Free Press*, June 24, 1876.

"Sundry Marine." *Detroit Free Press*, April 27, 1875.

U.S. Department of the Treasury, Bureau of Statistics. *List of Merchant Vessels of the United States*. U.S. Department of the Treasury: Washington, DC, 1869.

HARRY COULBY'S GRUESOME GIFT

"Beats Sailor, Is Jailed." *Detroit Free Press*, July 17, 1910.

"Buffalo Police Work New Lead." *Detroit Free Press*, July 13, 1910.

"Coulby, Harry—From Railway Worker to Shipping Magnate." Grantham Matters, August 12, 2012. GranthamMatters.co.uk.

"Ear Cutter Gets Long Prison Term." *Detroit Free Press*, November 22, 1910.

"Ear Cutter Is Guilty." *Detroit Free Press*, November 10, 1910.

"Ear Suspects Indicted." *Detroit Free Press*, September 21, 1910.

Havighurst, Walter. *Vein of Iron: The Pickands Mather Story*. Cleveland: World Publishing Company, 1958. https://catalog.hathitrust.org/Record/001107093.

"Marine Notes." *Detroit Free Press*, July 16, 1910.

"One Suspect Discharged." *Detroit Free Press*, September 15, 1910.

"Trace Owner of Ear." *Detroit Free Press*, July 12, 1910.

THROUGH THE WHEELHOUSE WINDOWS
OF THE *N. J. NESSEN*

"Accident to Worthington." *Detroit Free Press*, May 10, 1889.

American Lumberman, no. 2330. January 10, 1920.

"A Novel Experience." *Cleveland Plain Dealer*, July 13, 1900.

"Appeal to Inspectors." *Detroit Free Press*, May 4, 1904.

"A Propeller's Transformation." *Detroit Free Press*, April 15, 1886.

"Big Wrecking Job." *Manistee Daily Advocate*, April 26, 1907.

"Disappointment at Chicago." *Detroit Free Press*, May 9, 1904.

Hilton, George W. *The Great Lakes Car Ferries*. Berkeley, CA: Howell-North, 1962. https://
   archive.org/details/greatlakescarfer0000hilt.

"Lumber Carriers Ass'n." *Detroit Free Press*, May 7, 1904.

"Lumber Carriers Have Backed Down." *Detroit Free Press*, May 5, 1904.

"Lumber Carriers Signed a Contract." *Detroit Free Press*, May 8, 1904.

"Marine Notes." *Detroit Free Press*, May 13, 1883.

"Marine Notes." *Detroit Free Press*, June 24, 1884.

"Marine Notes." *Detroit Free Press*, June 4, 1885.

"Nessen Sinks in Two Minutes." *Manistee Daily Advocate*, April 11, 1907.

"Number Lost on Car Ferry Undetermined." *Milwaukee Sentinel*, October 22, 1929.

Public Health Reports: Supervising Surgeon General Marine Hospital Service. Vol. 14, nos. 1–52.
   Washington, DC: Government Printing Office, 1900.

"Shipwreck Impedes Marina Progress." *Leamington Post*, April 11, 1984.

"The Steambarge H. Luella Worthington." *Detroit Free Press*, June 9, 1880.

"Untitled." *Detroit Free Press*, July 15, 1880.

"Untitled." *Detroit Free Press*, July 24, 1880.

"Untitled." *Detroit Free Press*, July 27, 1880.

"Untitled." *Cleveland Plain Dealer*, April 15, 1886.

"Untitled." *Cleveland Plain Dealer*, April 9, 1907.

"Untitled." *Detroit Free Press*, October 24, 1929.

"Untitled." *Milwaukee Sentinel*, October 25, 1929.

"Waves Batter Helpless Ship." *Detroit News*, October 24, 1929.

THE ADVENT OF TANKERS ON THE GREAT LAKES

"An Oil Barge." *Detroit Free Press*, July 5, 1891.

"Another Oil Tank Launched." *Detroit Free Press*, June 5, 1895.

"Arrival From Europe." *Detroit Free Press*, June 12, 1861.

"Barge Iron City Crew Safe." *Detroit Free Press*, September 28, 1872.

"Barge Iron City Founders." *Detroit Free Press*, September 27, 1872.

"The Bartlett and the 55: Quick Work." *Detroit Free Press*, August 14, 1891.

Bascom, Jay, Toronto Marine Historical Society. Email to author, April 8, 2022.

"Blown Up." *Detroit Free Press*, July 12, 1890.

Boissoneault, Lorraine. "The Cuyahoga River Caught Fire at Least a Dozen Times, but No One Cared until 1969." *Smithsonian Magazine*, June 19, 2019. https://www.smithsonianmag.com.

"Cause of the Calamity." *Herald Democrat* (Leadville, CO), July 12, 1890.

Chernow, Ron. *Titan: The Life of John D. Rockefeller, Sr.* New York: Vintage Books, 1998.

"Direct Trade with Europe." *Detroit Free Press*, March 26, 1864.

"Disaster on the River." *Chicago Daily Inter-Ocean*, July 12, 1890.

"For Europe." *Detroit Free Press*, November 8, 1862.

"For Liverpool." *Chicago Tribune*, October 5, 1868.

Hidy, Ralph W., and Muriel E. Hidy. *Pioneering in Big Business: History of the Standard Oil Company (New Jersey), 1882–1911.* New York: Harper & Brothers, 1955.

"L. H. Cotton: Decided." *Chicago Tribune*, December 20, 1870.

"L. H. Cotton: Important Litigation." *Chicago Tribune*, December 19, 1870.

"Loss of the Barge Iron City." *Detroit Free Press*, September 27, 1872.

"Marine Mishaps." *Detroit Free Press*, October 9, 1877.

"Marine News." *Chicago Tribune*, October 27, 1868.

"Marine News." *Chicago Tribune*, October 31, 1868.

"Marine News." *Chicago Tribune*, December 20, 1870.

"Marine Notes." *Detroit Free Press*, August 13, 1872.

"Marine Notes." *Detroit Free Press*, June 16, 1875.

"Marine Notes." *Detroit Free Press*, August 22, 1878.

"Marine Notes." *Detroit Free Press*, August 31, 1878.

"Marine Notes." *Detroit Free Press*, July 30, 1891.

"Marine Notes." *Detroit Free Press*, May 1, 1895.

"Marine Notes." *Detroit Free Press*, May 12, 1895.

"Marine Notes." *Detroit Free Press*, May 14, 1895.

"Marine Notes." *Detroit Free Press*, July 12, 1895.

"Marine Notes." *Detroit Free Press*, July 21, 1895.

"Marine Notes." *Detroit Free Press*, July 25, 1895.

"Marine Notes." *Detroit Free Press*, September 10, 1895.

"Marine Notes." *Detroit Free Press*, November 6, 1895.

"Marine Notes." *Detroit Free Press*, May 8, 1902.

"Marine Notes." *Detroit Free Press*, November 12, 1902.

"Marine Notes." *Detroit Free Press*, April 24, 1903.

"Marine Notes." *Port Huron Daily Times*, December 2, 1903.

"Marine Notes." *Detroit Free Press*, August 2, 1911.

"Marine Notes." *Detroit Free Press*, October 31, 1911.

"Marine Notes." *Detroit Free Press*, July 7, 1912.

"Marine Notes." *Detroit Free Press*, July 20, 1912.

The Marine Review, June, 1911.

"Oil Barge Explodes." *Detroit Free Press*, May 2, 1912.

"Oil Cargo Is Condemned." *Detroit Free Press*, August 7, 1911.

"Oil for Liverpool." *Chicago Tribune*, October 19, 1868.

"On the Ocean." *Chicago Tribune*, October 30, 1868.

"One of the Oil Tanks Afloat." *Detroit Free Press*, June 29, 1895.

"The Petroleum Oil Trade." *Detroit Free Press*, October 14, 1862.

"Sailed for Europe." *Chicago Tribune*, October 8, 1868.

"Tank Ship Drops in at Collingwood." *Detroit Free Press*, December 16, 1915.

"The Tioga Calamity." *Detroit Free Press*, July 13, 1890.

"Vessel Passages." *Detroit Free Press*, September 24, 1911.

"Vessel Passages." *Detroit Free Press*, September 26, 1911.

Index